BROOKE BONEY, prnalist who has worked in radio tly on Nine's *Today* show. An com-municator, she also works as an MC, moderator, panellist and keynote speaker, with a huge passion for igniting discussion around Indigenous Affairs.

Brooke is currently studying a Masters of Public Policy at the University of Oxford. This is her first book.

Praise for *All of It*

'This book is warm, thoughtful and curious—just like Brooke.'
MIRANDA TAPSELL, actor and author

'Raw, funny, at times deeply emotional and so telling. Just magnificent . . . *All of It* delves into the very specific struggles Indigenous Australians face and why so much of that trauma is intergenerational. Brooke is an inspiration to me and I'm so proud to call her my dear friend. This book is important.'
ALLISON LANGDON, journalist and broadcaster

'*All of It* made me feel so proud to be Brooke's friend. Powerful and moving writing.'
TONY ARMSTRONG, host of *Eat the Invaders*

'Brooke Boney's voice has always been a sharp, lucid beacon in Australian journalism—combining thorough research with generosity, introspection and fearless honesty . . . From journalist and television presenter to columnist and cultural leader, Brooke has carved out a career that not only amplifies Aboriginal voices but also creates space for meaningful change. She makes the political personal with a striking ability to transform news and current affairs into human stories that resonate deeply and connect us all. Her insight, vision and talent are nothing short of extraordinary, and her voice will undoubtedly continue to echo far beyond the Australian literary landscape, leaving an indelible cultural impact.'

NAKKIAH LUI, award-winning writer

'Open, vulnerable, insightful, funny—*All of It* is truly all of it—and a brilliant read.'

JENNIFER ROBINSON, barrister and co-author of *How Many More Women?*

'Wow. Wow. Wow. A stunningly written meditation on fame, womanhood, Indigenous identity and the intersection of all three. Boney is an outstanding writer—every sentence is imbued with warmth and searing honesty. There are stories here that will stay with me forever. I can't recommend it highly enough.'

JESSIE STEPHENS, author of *Something Bad is Going to Happen*

All of It

All of II

All of It
Brooke Boney

Notes on public life, private joy and everything in between

First published in 2025

Copyright © Brooke Boney 2025

All rights reserved. No part of this book may be reproduced or transmitted in any form or by any means, electronic or mechanical, including photocopying, recording or by any information storage and retrieval system, without prior permission in writing from the publisher. The Australian *Copyright Act 1968* (the Act) allows a maximum of one chapter or 10 per cent of this book, whichever is the greater, to be photocopied by any educational institution for its educational purposes provided that the educational institution (or body that administers it) has given a remuneration notice to the Copyright Agency (Australia) under the Act.

Joan, an imprint of
Allen & Unwin
Cammeraygal Country
83 Alexander Street
Crows Nest NSW 2065
Australia
Phone: (61 2) 8425 0100
Email: info@allenandunwin.com
Web: www.allenandunwin.com

Allen & Unwin acknowledges the Traditional Owners of the Country on which we live and work. We pay our respects to all Aboriginal and Torres Strait Islander Elders, past and present.

 A catalogue record for this book is available from the National Library of Australia

ISBN 978 1 76106 800 3

Set in 13.35/21 pt Garamond Premier Pro by Midland Typesetters, Australia
Printed and bound in Australia by the Opus Group

10 9 8 7 6 5 4 3 2 1

 The paper in this book is FSC® certified. FSC® promotes environmentally responsible, socially beneficial and economically viable management of the world's forests.

*For Ann Marie, Dionne, Kirralai,
Ivy and Goldie. I love you.*

1.

Celebrity

On looking and being looked at

In a little over twelve hours from now, I'm going to resign from my job. The nerves are so intense that I've gone beyond feeling jittery or anxious and instead I just feel like I could faint. For the last few days I've been like this: catatonic. All I can do is lie on my bed and look at my phone like I'm waiting for the time to pass, even though I don't want to get any closer to the point when I have to tell the country I'm leaving.

I'm worried about how it will be perceived. I'm worried that there'll be spin put on it. I'm also maybe a little bit worried no one will care.

I go into work every day and talk to a camera. What I don't do is go into work every day and think about each person who is at home watching me, because if I did, I wouldn't be able to do it. I'd be a nervous wreck. Right now, though, I'm feeling the weight of every single one of those eyeballs. What will I say? How will I say it? Why am I even doing this?

Six years ago, I could never have predicted being where I am right now, about to leave my job as a TV journalist and go study overseas at Oxford University. It's beyond any goal I'd set for myself, or anything I thought I'd be capable of doing or invited to do.

I remember I was sitting at a pub in Paddington in November or December 2018, about to host a talk for Helen McCabe and her organisation Future Women, when I got a missed call from a man named Steven Burling. Helen saw the notification on my phone and, knowing Steven had just been given the job as director of morning TV at Channel 9, said, 'You probably want to call him back as soon as you can.' That phone call would change my life in ways that I could never have imagined. A few weeks later I signed a contract to appear on the breakfast TV show *Today*, where I'd work for the next six years.

And now I am about to resign.

I never really understood Australia's fascination with breakfast TV. But I still absorbed plenty of it by osmosis; I've known who the hosts of *Today* are for as long as I can remember. In more recent years—before I was on the show—I also learned details about their lives that I really shouldn't have. I recall sitting in the press gallery in Parliament House one afternoon when I saw a tweet from Lisa Wilkinson saying she was leaving the show. I remember when Karl Stefanovic got engaged to Jas, too. I can't imagine I was the intended audience for any of that information—before I started at Channel 9, I was a newsreader at triple j, working horrendous hours deep in the bowels of the ABC. But at some point during the long workdays, I obviously clicked on those dishy headlines.

Is this collective fascination with the lives of breakfast TV hosts because Australia doesn't have the same sort of celebrity culture as in the US or the UK, so there aren't as many people to write about?

As I lie on my bed, waiting for the hour of my resignation, I'm looking around at all the stuff I've accumulated since I left the comfort of the tiny country town of Muswellbrook eighteen years ago—stuff that at the time I felt like I desperately needed, but that I'll now have to rehome or throw out. Stuff that cost money, which I had to work incredibly hard for. I had to wake up early to make that money!

Has it even been worth it? Does having all this stuff make up for missing birthdays and Christmases and weddings and funerals? Or not being able to take calls or nurse babies or understand in-jokes, because I wasn't there when they started? I can't say for sure either way.

What about the work I've done? Will it mean anything to anyone once I'm not on TV every single day? Do clout and notoriety deteriorate if you're not constantly building on them? I've been on national radio or TV every weekday except for holidays since 2017, helping Australians wake up and go about their day. It's hard to comprehend that. It's like trying to imagine a single molecule and the entire solar system at the same time.

One of my closest friends once painted me for the Archibald Prize, and it was such a nice painting that we both thought she might win. It wasn't nice because it was of me, but because it was beautiful and pink and there was a dog in it—and because she's so incredibly talented. They hung prints of the painting everywhere around the city, on light posts and pillars from William Street all the way down to Circular Quay. One day I was catching a car into town, and I saw the image hanging ten metres tall on a post next to Hyde Park. I thought, *oh wow, that's me. That's a painting of me, and I'm driving past it. Is this what it feels like to be famous?*

I've always thought there are levels to fame, and that some of them are more pleasant than others. For example, you'd want enough fame to get invited to nice places, but not enough to get bothered when you go to the supermarket. It'd be nice for people to know your name but to not always know your face.

Celebrity

They'd say things like, 'Oh, you put me in mind of someone,' or 'Have we met before?'

We all feel so close to the influencers and celebrities we follow. But really we're so far away, just sitting at home, rotting in our beds like we've got a Victorian-era wasting disease, scrolling on these little devices that give us the perception of having unfettered access to everyone and anyone in the world at any time of the day. But we don't. It's all very contrived, and even authenticity can be fabricated if you've got people around you who are clever enough to help you maintain the facade. There are elements of how celebrity is manufactured that are really quite insidious and disturbing. During my decade-long media career, I've seen the disturbing parts up close a number of times.

Once, I noticed a car following me home from work. It wasn't the first time, and it wouldn't be the last. This kind of thing creates a pattern that makes you feel like you could be losing your mind, a kind of paranoia that is amplified by a lack of sleep and trauma from having been stalked in the past. You're aware of details that others don't notice, because they might not even be real. You'd be surprised how easily someone sitting in the front seat of a car and drinking from a big water bottle can be mistaken for a photographer with a long-range lens—something my co-hosts and I have laughed about in the past.

Anyway, this time when I was followed home, the car tracked me from the Channel 9 car park towards the highway and onto the Sydney Harbour Bridge. It's quite a specific route, so as I drew closer to home, it felt less and less likely that someone else would be taking the exact same path as me. When I pulled into the lane next to me, the other car did the same. When I got to Moore Park Road, I decided to test it further. I signalled left and deviated from my normal route. Seconds later, so did the driver in the car I was watching.

By then I was scared. No one who wishes you well follows you home from work. Who was this person? Was it a stalker? A pap? Maybe they were a crazed viewer who didn't like what I had to say about January 26 and wanted to let me know in person. After all, there were plenty of people who threatened to do just that. Eventually, I called the network publicist, who told me to either go to a shopping centre or the police station, but to avoid going home, as whoever was following me would then know where I lived. The way he said it was so routine, which isn't to say that he was being casual about the situation, more that it was definitely advice he'd given out before. But for me, I never thought I'd hear something like that outside of a movie about a kidnapping.

I was terrified. And then I thought, *fuck it, why am I running away from an invisible enemy? If they want to hurt me, they're going to, so I might as well confront them.* I got to Bondi Junction and slammed my brakes on, then pulled over on the side of the road and got out of the car. The guy chucked a U-turn and pulled up across the road, but he jumped straight out of his car and I couldn't see him anywhere. As I surveyed his car, I thought seriously about smashing his windscreen, weighing up the potential consequences, before my better judgement prevailed. Then the driver emerged from the bushes down the street. He was a photographer. A pap.

I said to him, 'Do you know how terrified I am right now? What gives you the right to follow a woman home from work?'

All he said was, 'You're in this world now. It's a part of the job.'

'I thought you were going to hurt me,' I told him. 'Doesn't that make you feel bad?'

He was undeterred. 'Just let me get a photo and I'll leave you alone.'

So I walked away from him, heading down the street and back again, pretending to be on the phone.

Before he got back into his car, the pap said, 'By the way, thanks for all of the work you do in the diversity space.'

Can you believe that?

To his credit, he later sent me a message on Instagram, saying that he acknowledged our interaction must have been uncomfortable and that if I ever wanted to be papped, I could let him know. That does happen, by the way. A publicist or celebrity will tip off paps and tell them where to be at a particular time if they want to get a photo of a specific moment for a specific story. Photographers show up for these 'candid' shoots or try to catch people off guard because they can flog the photos off to a publication for a few hundred dollars and make a quick buck. I guess there are worse ways to make money.

I've been stalked for nearly all my adult life. It's unsettling, cruel and a cowardly way to impose power over someone without having to interact with them at all. From what I can tell, for the most part stalkers fall into two categories: the fixated kind or the crazy kind. They're either obsessed with you, or they're obsessed with your ability to help them draw attention to a story or a cause.

When I worked at triple j, I smoked cigarettes, and I would stand out the front of the ABC building between news bulletins, indulging in a lung lolly. One time, a man I didn't recognise walked over to me and said, 'I can't believe you're not going to say anything to me.' He seemed slighted that I didn't acknowledge him right away, like we were old friends from school and I'd deliberately snubbed him. I pride myself on remembering people and their circumstances, but my short-term memory is also terrible, mainly because I never get enough sleep due to the early alarms I set to go to work. So I assumed that we must have known each other and I'd just forgotten who he was. Even though it would have been unusual for me to forget, it wasn't impossible.

I quickly realised he wasn't well once I started talking to him; he was jittery and tense like someone who had somewhere to be, but he was unkempt and presented weirdly. My brain could recognise something was amiss but not from a few metres away and not soon enough for him to get within centimetres of me. So I ran towards the security guards at the front door of the building. I told them what just happened, and they ran out to speak to the man, but he'd already fled.

When I got back into the studio, we looked at the triple j textline and realised the same man had been trying to reach out to beg me to cover a story on the news. Then I checked my Facebook inbox and saw he'd been trying to reach me there as well. It went on for weeks. I spent hours at the police station, giving them a statement and arranging for ways to safely travel to and from work. The man would go on to return to the location multiple times before the police eventually caught up with him, and when they did, he threw a cup of his own urine onto them as they arrested him. I don't know what stories he wanted me to cover but apparently he wanted to give the cup to me so we could run some tests. It seems like he was having some sort of psychotic episode and maybe thought he was being poisoned.

A couple of years later, I moved into a terrace where I lived on my own while I waited for my boyfriend to return home from studying overseas. In the middle of the night, I kept hearing loud bangs and what could only be described as footsteps throughout the house. I will concede that I am easily spooked, and as I mentioned earlier, I'm quite prone to paranoia when I haven't had enough sleep. Everyone dismissed my concerns, saying that what I was hearing was likely just the noises of an old house I wasn't yet used to. My boyfriend suggested that I have a friend sleep in the spare room until he returned home. So I did, and the presence of another human in the house massively helped.

One night, though, my friend and I were both sleeping when an almighty *thud* came from downstairs. It was loud enough to wake us both up. I got a text: 'Did you hear that?' 'Yes', I replied. Assured by the text and our mutual fear and paranoia, I went back to sleep, and a few hours later I woke to go to work. I showered and pottered about the house for a bit, then left. A few hours later, my friend did the same.

When I returned from work at 10 a.m., the back garage was open, which was unusual because the only way to open it was with a remote, which was attached to the house keys—on a keyring, which we kept inside the house. Then, as I walked towards the back of the house to look at the garage, I noticed the wood on the back door had been chipped away, like someone had tried to jimmy it open. I immediately called the police, and they came and took statements and fingerprinted the surfaces around the doors. It all seemed pretty straightforward: they'd check in on the aforementioned stalker to make sure he wasn't in the area at the time and run any fingerprints they'd collected through their database to see if they could find out who might've been at our house.

But as I sat at the kitchen table near the back door, one of the officers who was staring at the marks on the door said, 'Brooke, I don't think this is someone trying to get into the house. I think these marks are from the inside. Someone was trying to get out.'

My stomach sank. I felt violated. A stranger had been inside my house with me while I was sleeping. While I was showering. While I was pottering about. I had security cameras installed, but despite their best efforts, the police never found any clues as to who had broken in. So whoever it was, they're still out there somewhere.

More recently, another incident ended with me taking out an AVO on someone because they kept showing up at my work and wouldn't leave, despite being told that I wouldn't see them and that I wasn't interested in hearing what they had to say. But the AVO only happened after many sleepless nights and many hours spent with police trying to figure out a resolution.

I must add that these experiences are not unique; they have probably happened to most of the people you follow who have a public profile. I know it's a bit sick, but I find a tiny piece of comfort in knowing that it hasn't just affected me. After the last incident left me panicked and riddled with anxiety, my younger sister, who is infinitely smarter and wiser than me, said, 'You can let this destroy you and be scared of shadows for the rest of your life, or you can learn how to fight and move on.' So I learned how to fight, taking self-defence lessons each Friday after work, and looked into buying pepper spray off the internet.

If things like this have happened to me this many times, imagine how much it must happen when you're *really* famous. I wonder if Beyoncé had to learn how to fight or when she last went to a supermarket. Do you think she misses it? I would if I was her. You wouldn't even know what kinds of yoghurt or dip they have these days. What a tragedy that would be: missing out on coconut yoghurt or dips with layers of sour cream, salsa and guacamole.

But who knows? Maybe she does go to the supermarket. Once I was doing groceries at World Square in Sydney, and this guy came over to me and said, 'Oh, I thought you'd have people to do that for you!' I could've made a joke about firing them because they got the wrong dip. I wish I'd thought of that at the time.

Celebrity

There is an episode of *The Kardashians* where Kris and Kylie go to the shops. They kind of fumble about and don't know how to go through the checkout properly, and they think the whole thing is hilarious. This is the stage we're at: we'll watch someone cosplaying as a normal person, pretending to be just like us and laughing about doing things we have no choice but to do and maybe even enjoy. The Kardashians' shopping trip feels a bit undignified to me, like they're insulting us. It's like laughing at people who clean up your mess, or at a waiter who endures humiliation for a tip. But we let the Kardashians do it. We watch their shows and buy their products while they mock us in this way.

We really do love pap shots of famous people doing their groceries. Whether it's Natalie Portman or Billie Eilish, we just want to see a photo of a beautiful person struggling behind the weight of their trolley so that we feel better about having to do it too. Those are the shots that probably aren't set up. But whether we are watching genuinely candid private moments or entirely staged scenes for reality TV or publicity, we can't get enough of them.

Therein lies the problem. It doesn't matter which side of the dynamic you're on, whether you're the voyeur or the exhibitionist: fame is a machine and it's a hungry beast with an insatiable appetite for content. Those who cannot fathom fading into obscurity continue to feed it.

Knowing what I know about the pressure that comes with maintaining a public profile, I do wonder how anyone participating in the circus manages to cling to any level of sanity. In the age of social media, people are desperate to misunderstand you, prove you wrong or expose some kind of hypocrisy. They want you to slip up and show a side of yourself that is uncomfortable and perhaps a bit grotesque.

There's a quote from one of my favourite authors, Arundhati Roy, that I think helps to explain the yearning some people have for fame and overachieving: 'And she had learned from experience that Need was a warehouse that could accommodate a considerable amount of cruelty.' If you have a need for admiration or attention maybe that means your threshold or endurance is greater than others.

I guess that's part of the reason I'm pulling the ripcord: I don't have the constitution to be a person with a profile anymore. It's all too much to bear. The constant scrutiny, the charade you have to maintain to keep it all together, the tightrope walk between vulnerability and relatability and 'protecting your energy'. It's not *just* that I feel like it's undignified.

I just don't want it badly enough to keep putting myself under this much pressure. I've been waking up before the sunrise for all my thirties—a time when you should be staying out past sunrise. I've been so committed to overcoming my

Celebrity

circumstances that I just can't stop working. Is this meant to be a measure of my usefulness to the world? Is it proof to throw in the face of every person who questions the work ethic of black people? Perhaps it's redemption for everyone who's ever underestimated me, or others like me? Or maybe it's revenge for those who couldn't see me when I wanted to be seen and respected? I don't know. All I know is that it's unnatural, and in my darker moments I think it's kind of unholy. The reason for this overworking is as much a mystery to me as the ability to wake up at 3.15 a.m. is to night owls. I don't know. It just happens.

I can't figure out why I push myself so hard. Pop always said to us that as Aboriginal people if we wanted to be considered equal we had to be the best, and I guess I took that literally and to the nth degree. I always had so much admiration and respect for Pop, and so did the broader community. He was right; we weren't assigned the same value as others at birth, so we do have to work hard to prove we deserve to exist at all. If our lives aren't intrinsically worthy, then at least we can contribute in a way that means we are economically valuable to society if nothing else.

Feeling understood, proving something to one's parents or enemies, redemption or fortune—whatever the need that lies behind it, being famous can only be achieved when there's a force at play that is greater than anything immediately obvious to the normal observer, propelling one forward and continuing the momentum. Fame is a business that's too complex to navigate and a greater but more insidious force, too humiliating to endure for the sake of celebrity in and of itself. Politicians fall prey to these same forces: Churchill wanted to please his father, while the Obamas were driven to push civil rights forward.

Lifting the veil on this secret of celebrity feels like it could be grounds for being exiled. It's like the more difficult parts of the industry should be a closely held secret, otherwise people might not aspire to be famous and it'll no longer be something that people desire. The jig will be up.

The problem is that when you're motivated by these powerful forces, they create a hunger that, much like the public's need for distraction, will never be satiated. More will never be enough. I bet Taylor Swift doesn't wake up and think, *okay, well, I've got seven albums in the top ten and I'm a billionaire, so maybe that's enough*. I don't think Meghan Markle goes to bed thinking, *wow, I was a princess, and now I've got two beautiful children and an adoring husband. What more could I possibly want?*

In the past, when a celebrity did a publicity tour and came to Australia to promote their new album or movie, only certain outlets would be given access: *Today* or *Sunrise*, a couple of FM radio stations, and maybe a magazine or a newspaper. If all went to plan and the anecdotes landed and the celebrity in question was the perfect mix of humble and entertaining, they'd sell out their shows and get to number one on the charts, or they'd have a stellar opening weekend at the box office. That's how it has worked for decades upon decades.

But promotion of music and films has shifted dramatically. Since the Covid-19 pandemic, our obsession with our phones and social media has exponentially increased, and our infatuation with celebrity culture has reached fever pitch. The way that cultural products—be they movies, songs or celebrities themselves—are marketed now is so much more sophisticated that you'd need a Harvard MBA and some sort of NASA calculator to figure out the perfect formula. And there's not a single artist in the world right now who is able to compete with the strategy employed by Taylor Swift.

Swift's marketing machine is a self-perpetuating monster, with multiple parts working in perfect harmony to continue to propel her career, status and wealth ad infinitum. Her team employs a genius kind of strategy centred around not only appeasing an adoring fan base to push her music to the top of the charts and sell out shows and merchandise, but also teasing that same fan base, coercing them deeper into their obsession. If you've never looked at online forums or groups dedicated to worshipping celebrities like Swift, please do yourself a favour and have a little peek. There are grown men and women with serious jobs and children to look after who spend their precious finite time devoted to worshipping someone they have never met and probably never will. Their devotion isn't to her, but to an idea that they've projected onto a stranger based on clever marketing and performance.

I don't mean to diminish Swift's contribution to pop culture by pointing out the power of the machine she's built around her. The connection felt by millions of people with her music and brand of proud girlhood seems genuine. These people must yearn for a full expression of the experiences that they feel have been quelled or silenced by society.

In my family, we are all guilty of mocking the trademarks of girlhood while simultaneously celebrating boyhood. Even though we love our niece and nephew equally, we'll poke fun at the fact that my beautiful little niece does silly dances and bakes and likes to film it all so she can share it on TikTok. (Her follower base is made up solely of our family members.) We joke about how we can't wait to share the videos at her 21st birthday, and we don't take her aspirations seriously. At the same time, we'll celebrate my nephew's achievements on the football field and speak of his strength and valour, imagining what kind of career he could carve out and how much bigger and more skilful he'll get as he grows up.

If what Swift is offering is an opportunity for women and girls to be unashamedly themselves, rather than masking their identities and feelings or feigning interest in more male-dominated hobbies, then that is fantastic. But I think we can say the relationship between Swift and her fans goes beyond a bond of mutual enjoyment at expressing their unmet childhood desires. Well beyond that.

In a February 2024 ABC article, one of Australia's sharpest political minds, Leigh Sales, turned her hand to trying to decipher exactly what it is that makes Swift so appealing to her audiences:

> My first theory is that her appeal is tied to what I noted right at the start: she's not the best at anything. She's fantastic at everything of course, but not the best at any one of the individual skills that make a great artist. That means she's not some god-like object of worship to her fans, she's just Tay Tay and that makes her more accessible.
>
> Take the choreography at the Eras show for example. The moves are sexy but she doesn't land them in a sexy way, although she appears to be trying. She lands them in a way that is somehow reminiscent of you and your best friend at school trying to land Madonna's Vogue routine but still looking like your own goofy, nerdy selves.

The way Sales describes Swift is interesting: she's relatable. There are those who say she sometimes dresses badly on purpose. She makes you feel okay about yourself. I would argue, however, that perhaps she's only relatable to those who are like her in some way. I'm not a fan of leaning into identity politics, but I do think it's worth pointing out this blind spot. I'm sure she is a lovely person, perhaps even with wonderful intentions, but feminism that is not intersectional leaves behind the most vulnerable women. If our intention is to create a more equitable future, then surely it shouldn't come with an asterisk that qualifies who gets to be a part of it and who doesn't.

For better or worse, we look to celebrities for moral guidance and they indulge us. When it comes to Taylor Swift, we cannot bury our heads in the sand and pretend that a full and unfettered expression of girlhood is the most pressing or important feminist issue, particularly when women and girls across the world are facing unprecedented levels of violence and repression, contraception is impossible to access for many women in developing countries, and the practice of female genital mutilation is still occurring in some parts of the world. In the United States—Swift's home country—women do not have full bodily autonomy or reproductive rights in all territories. Girlhood is important and worth celebrating, but not at the expense of more serious and urgent issues affecting women. That's not to say you can't focus on progressing one area within your control and neglect the others—no one person can do everything on their own—but it is uncomfortable to witness someone ignoring the more contentious issues while basking in the goodwill and compliments of the public because they create an environment where people can be themselves. I know it's not just Swift who steers clear, and she did eventually endorse Kamala Harris in the 2024 US election. At the very least, silence from celebrities suggests they are ignorant about these issues affecting women; at worst, it suggests they don't care enough to use their platform to speak about topics that are controversial or only impact minorities, perhaps because of the financial or reputational cost it might incur. But what is the point of reaching the milestone of billionairedom if not to do that very thing? Is it to be the best? To be the richest? It warrants scrutiny.

So much of celebrity culture is rooted in flaunting wealth. Huge houses, huge lips, huge asses. Everything is big and getting bigger. If there was more literacy around economics and the finite nature of resources, then people might realise that by even consuming content created by these people—let alone buying their products—we're playing an active role in disparity by contributing to their wealth while simultaneously draining our own. If this relationship was explained to people in a way that made sense, would they still take part in the transactions?

Is it a matter of wanting to look at nice pictures of people and emulate their dress sense or their hair and make-up styles? Are we really trying to emulate a perception of wealth, despite the fact that we've just become less rich by carrying out some of these transactions? I like reading comments on these braggadocious posts—engagement is a form of currency as much as time spent listening, or buying merchandise. One time I saw a comment that said, 'You should be humble with your blessings,' and I thought, *wow, I guess not everyone's buying it.*

At this juncture where celebrity worship has reached fever pitch, we really ought to consider why it is that we'd take ethical direction from people who are good at singing and acting. I imagine the same parts of culture idolised by the more vacuous corners of the internet have also aided in shifting us away from values rooted in our shared humanity and community. Perhaps it's also that a lack of belief or trust in politicians, faith and community leaders created a vacuum that's been occupied by entertainers and influencers—people who, in most cases, are concerned more with broad appeal than providing substantial moral or ethical guidance informed by years of experience, education and soul searching. It's not just a lack of wisdom that disqualifies some celebrities from holding such important spaces and roles, but their intentions. Mass appeal and commercial reward are not ideal starting points or fertile ground for spiritual and thought leaders who will steer us to a destination other than the one we're headed towards—one that is governed by those concerned more with oppressive individualism than with freedom and fairness for all.

I know this sounds cynical, and I'm aware that there is magic in music and performance. I've also been guilty of celebrity worship at certain times. When I was younger, I was convinced that I would someday marry Taylor Hanson if only I could meet him. Then he would feel what I felt, and our connection would be guaranteed! Granted, I was ten years old, and the only interaction I'd had with him was watching clips on *Video Hits* and reading interviews in magazines like *Smash Hits*. Nevertheless, I was convinced we had a future together.

Marketing artists in those days must have been so much easier than it is now. Nowadays, if an artist says something political in an interview, it might go viral, and then there's a chance they'll be cancelled. They could be accused of any number of sins: queerbaiting, blackfishing, political ambivalence. They could have a photo snapped by a fellow diner at a restaurant that makes them look like a mere mortal. Or they could have some historical, out-of-context tweets dug up that would wipe the sheen from their brand.

But while we have these intrusive behaviours from the public that go well beyond what is appropriate and sometimes beyond what is legal, we also have a group of people who yearn for relevance. So where are the boundaries? And how much sympathy should we have for those who fly dangerously close to the line in order to benefit their finances and reputation?

People dream of stardom and aspire to fame and fortune, until they have it. So often we hear of celebrities who live in gated communities far away from the adoring public and any real scrutiny. It reminds me of one of my friend's favourite sayings: 'Be careful what you wish for, because you just might get it.'

I've seen celebrities up close in interviews, and they do get nervous when they are required to speak to journalists to promote their movies. To be honest, it's quite endearing to see someone who's won an Oscar reduced to an anxious mess. I don't mean that I like to see people suffer; it's just that the more you see their humanity, the more 'relatable' famous people are. I guess that's why it's recently become popular for celebrities to release their own documentaries; they have far greater control over the edit while still providing their fans with a sense of intimacy and familiarity. This choice is more than understandable in a culture where the public wants relatability but will shun their idols when they see their flaws or hear them make a controversial statement.

Now this is when I call myself out as a hypocrite—I'm party

to these transactions too. Just last week a package arrived at my home. Inside the beautiful box were two smaller boxes wrapped in tissue paper and finished with matte cardboard in muted tones. Each box was adorned with a chic font spelling out the names of all the exotic oils and scents contained within. And the products? They can only be described as the most indulgent and expensive hair care I've ever bought.

The package came from a brand called Cécred. It's Beyoncé's haircare line, which is designed for people with curly hair and was made specifically with black women in mind. I think I would be lying if I said I bought it for those (quite practical) reasons though. No, I bought it because Beyoncé uses it, and I want to know how she makes her hair look so perfect. I'm also kind of curious about what she smells like—and I guess now I know, because it's what I smell like too. I'm too ashamed to tell you what the package cost, but just know that it's more than what makes sense in this economy, and if I was thinking clearly, I would've split the shipping with my friends who also wanted the products but sensibly baulked at the price. What's the saying about having more money than sense? Turns out the threshold for this ratio isn't that high after all, particularly when it comes to celebrity-marketed haircare products and my willingness to support those who align with my identity and my politics.

If this is a hypocrisy mea culpa, then I might as well keep the ball rolling. I am guilty of looking at pap shots even though I know how intrusive and awful it feels when those photos are taken.

I scoured and studied the photos of Kate Middleton that were released during her absence from public life after she'd had abdominal surgery. I called friends to talk about what we thought might've been going on. And like everyone else on the internet, I felt guilty when it was revealed she'd been diagnosed with cancer and would be treated with chemotherapy.

No doubt the case of Kate's disappearance was highly intriguing and garnered a lot of public interest—but why? Was it because the public relations machine that has managed to hold together the British monarchy for centuries, upholding their dominance over much of the globe, had begun to show cracks? For a moment, it seemed as though they might not be able to navigate a digital-first world with all the increased scrutiny of people in positions of power that entails. Traditionally, the Royal Family has maintained their trademark 'keep calm and carry on' visage because of their close, mutually beneficial relationships with royal reporters and watchers. But as they quickly learnt in 2024, people on the internet do not follow the same rules.

Celebrity

To some extent, information about the health of the successors to the throne of the Commonwealth is in the public interest, but a lot of what I saw and read in the weeks Kate was absent was gratuitous, salacious and, at times, cruel. While celebrities like Beyoncé and Taylor Swift have figured out that in order to appease their fans they should overshare and oversupply content, the strategy of the Royals to 'never complain and never explain' left an information vacuum—one that, if it couldn't be filled by the truth, would be filled by far-fetched conspiracy theories. Whether that is fair or not is not for me to decide, but it is how marketing works in this modern age, no matter whether you're Queen Bey or Princess Kate.

Is this the reason people in the United States turn celebrities like Beyoncé and Taylor Swift into royalty—because they don't have their own monarchy? And is this why breakfast TV hosts are celebrities in Australia—because we don't have Beyoncé and Taylor Swift? After all, their positions in society are all built on the same general principles: power, wealth and, in some cases, notoriety.

The public's willingness and hunger to tear down people who they perceive to be above them is nothing new. In Australia we call it tall poppy syndrome. If someone sticks their neck out, then we come together as a mob and delight in chopping them down. I'd like to think there is something noble about it, a yearning for life's misfortunes to be shared equally, but it's more likely that it's just spiteful. We don't want people having access to what we think we deserve.

This is why it takes bravery to say things that are unpopular even if you think you're right. It's also why I'm not as sad to leave broadcasting as some might think I should be. It's a huge responsibility.

There's a reason people put themselves through all of this despite the drawbacks: if you do it right and you do it well, then it affords you a certain freedom. To be brutally honest, I complain a lot about the pressure of having a public profile for someone with such a small public profile. But some people are more comfortable with this lifestyle than others. Some people seem to even enjoy the parts that I find uncomfortable, like getting dressed up and going to red carpet events or to the races. Even though I can't count myself among them, I know that by doing this job I've been able to support my family in ways I never dreamed were possible. I've seen more of the world than I would have otherwise, and in the same way that I felt the veil had been lifted on government while I was working in Parliament House, I've been able to see behind the scenes of the entertainment industry too. The more talented people are, the more money they can make for themselves and the people around them, and the more power they hold. At the moment, that power seems to be predominantly in the hands of women like Beyoncé, Taylor Swift and Chappell Roan—and that should be cause for celebration.

I don't think I'm done proving my worth or striving for more. But now, for the first time in a long time, I'm going to be able to wake up with the sun and not before it. I'm going to be able to go out to dinner during the week and not have to ask my friends to eat at 5.30 p.m. I'm going to be able to click on articles about morning TV and not wonder if I'm the subject of them.

I recently had a conversation with someone who has a much bigger public profile than me about whether it's possible to press rewind or reset on being a public figure.

I guess I'm about to find out.

2.

Ghost Stories

On mothers, grandmothers and what we inherit

'My mother's gifts of courage to me were both large and small. The latter are woven so subtly into the fabric of my psyche that I can hardly distinguish where she stops and I begin.'

Maya Angelou, *Mom & Me & Mom*

Some hours change your life and how you think about yourself more than an entire decade can. They can either make you feel whole or pick apart everything you know to be certain. They can unravel everything or make everything make sense.

You know how in every family there are myths about things that happened a long time ago? Failed marriages, illegitimate children, secret jobs. The myths exist as ghosts, whispers from other rooms in your home, and they are hushed as soon as it seems like they might become real. These stories are so opaque and intangible that investigating them feels like trying to extract a brain tumour—one of the ones that doesn't have edges or real substance, just a gooey mass without a membrane, moving between crevices in your brain and growing until it prevents everything from operating how it's supposed to. Family myths sometimes have the same effect: they maim, numb and gag us.

My family's myth is woven so tightly with the secrets of the nation that for a long time it was almost a crime to talk about it. It certainly was a crime to talk about it in your own language, which I guess is the language spoken by our ghosts and ancestors. Picking at the seams of these family and national myths can land you in prison or a mental hospital, which is where this story ends.

For a long time, children who looked like me, with green eyes and big smiles and skin that wasn't quite white but wasn't quite black, were taken away from their mothers. Children who played in the creeks while their mothers watched. Children who ate damper and dripping and were given rations.

When the children were taken, they were told they weren't loved, because everyone who had ever loved them had died or didn't want them anymore. They were told their names were different from the ones they were given by the people who used to love them. They were physically and sexually abused, and they were forced to work as slaves for people with fairer skin and more luck. Can you imagine anything more terrifying than that? That was their ghost story. But what made it all the more scary was that it was real. And it happened all the time.

Ghost Stories

Like a storm approaching on the horizon of the northwest plains of New South Wales, the arrival of these ghosts was announced by the dirt and dust kicked up by government cars driving out towards the missions on the outskirts of town. They snaked their way towards those places where the black people and their brown children were condemned to during daylight hours. Every child would try to outrun and hide from the ghosts, to avoid being taken away and given a new name. No one wants a new name, especially if you already have a beautiful one.

My great-grandmother had one of the most beautiful names of all: Nola. Nanny Nola. It's supposed to mean something about being white, fair and beautiful, which feels especially cruel as the colour of her skin is what sealed her fate. It's also my name—Brooke Nola—so I carry her with me everywhere. She is part of me, and I am part of her. We think of our home country in the same way. That's what we call our native lands. Our home country. Even the sound of that phrase ushers in a feeling of belonging for me. Leaving home. Coming home. No matter how far you stray, it is where you belong.

Every black person has these stories about government cars snaking out and bringing the ghost clouds with them to take away the children, but Nanny Nola's story is different. Yes, they came to get the children, but this one particular day, at one particular hour—an hour that, for her, had more of an impact than the decades that came before or after—it wasn't the ghosts who took the babies and their names and their futures. Still, in that one particular moment, Nanny Nola lost her mother and her baby sibling, and our family—the McGradys and then the Boneys—would always feel the impact. We would feel it even before we were what we were, and we'd feel it even if we didn't really know it. We'd feel it in the ways we were mothered and the ways we mothered. We are forever haunted by the cruelty inflicted on our forebears.

Nanny Nola was a baby in the 1930s, before we were considered human in New South Wales. I can't imagine how our home country looked then. I don't know if people looked at our babies during that period and thought they were beautiful like they do now.

I also don't know exactly where she was. I don't know exactly when any of this happened. I don't know, because I could never quite hear the whispers through the walls, and it's a shame so shameful that no one ever wanted to talk about it in the open. So, eventually, the details were lost.

What I do know is that when they came to take the babies and all the children ran to find their hiding places, one baby was still with Nanny Nola's mother. In her desperation to be invisible and silent as the ghosts were hunting, her mother muffled the baby's cries until there was no more breath to hide and no more crying to muffle. So instead of the children being taken away that day, Nanny Nola's mother was. She went crazy and was locked up in a mental institution in the city, where she would stay until she died in the 1990s.

I've always known that was part of our story. I've also always wanted to know more, but I felt that it was a spot too tender to touch. It's been something that connected me to the terrible history of this country and the impact of colonisation, but it felt so distant and a truth so difficult to grasp that it turned into a family myth: rarely spoken of or acknowledged, and barely remembered in the decades that followed.

In those same decades, I shared a bed with my Nanny Nola after I ran away from home to live with my grandparents. I remember her long fingernails tenderly scratching my scalp as we'd watch TV together with the air conditioner blaring, while her daughter—my nan—cooked us rissoles and vegetables or spaghetti bolognese. That was my idea of peak comfort and contentment: refuge from the cruel world and the Muswellbrook heat, a poor person's feast, and my Nanny Nola.

Every day before school, Nanny Nola would ask me where I was going at least twice. Maybe she had some symptoms of the early stages of dementia, or maybe she knew that I was going to wag and go to my friend's house to smoke cigarettes all day and wanted to suss me out.

Like dust in the wind, our memories fade and then settle, and the further in time you get away from the bad things that happen, the less people remember and the less real it becomes. That is, of course, until you see your great-grandmother fighting to draw her final breaths. Then you realise that, for some people, the myths were never myths. Everything was real. The ghosts weren't ghosts at all; they were white men who came to take them away. These are their lives and their stories, but the only way we interact with them now is through a lens of trauma.

For some reason, this trauma revealed itself to me the last time I saw my namesake, Nanny Nola, alive. I've heard stories about people seeing a black dog in the room with them as they approach the end of their lives. Apparently it seems as real as anything else in the room, and they shriek and cry and get scared and ask their carers and family members to get rid of the dog. But no one can help them, because the dog's not there. My great-grandmother didn't see the dog, but she did stuff a blanket in her mouth. She started saying something about taking the babies. She was crying and shaking and dying. I didn't know what to do to alleviate her suffering, so I just sat there and patted her frail, veiny hand and cried along with her. A little chorus of cries.

I think she was reliving her sibling's final moments with her mother.

In that particular hour of that particular day, when for some reason it was just the two of us together, it dawned on me that she would've felt that guilt her whole life. My beautiful, tender, loving great-grandmother, who loved me for no reason other than that's what grandparents are supposed to do, was riddled with guilt, walking around with secrets her whole life long. In that moment, I realised the depths black women must plunge to in order to summon the will to get through every day. And they do it for their babies, so they can run their fingers through our hair. So they can love us for no reason.

It's the greatest loss I've ever felt, having a merry love like that go quiet. She was the last person to love me simply because I'm nice and kind and sweet. I know this is true, because she started losing her mind before I achieved anything.

You can never really be certain if anyone loves you for you—if they can separate you from your achievements or your potential or what they might be able to gain from your potential. The only way you can know is if they loved you before any of it ever happened. Before any of it was ever thought of. When you are at your worst and no one has a clue yet about what your best could be. And still they are there, loving you anyway.

I remember being invited for supper at the Governor General's house in Kirribilli to mark Harmony Day. It seemed counterintuitive to me that there'd be any harmony to be found in inviting members of marginalised communities to eat with the same cutlery used by the princes and princesses of the British monarchy when they come to visit the colony.

When I sat down—before the Governor General's wife was seated, which is absolutely not allowed—I remember examining all the cutlery laid out. I was immediately drawn back into my childhood, when my grandmother would invite my cousins and I over and teach us how to take tea properly. She'd lay out cutlery on a long table and put the tea and biscuits and cakes in the middle, with little jars of sugar to sweeten the brew. My guess is that she would've been taught this ritual by Nanny Nola, who worked as a domestic servant in a house in Sydney.

That they squirrelled away these little nuggets of tradition and information so they could pass them on, just in case one of their granddaughters got invited to sit with the Queen or her representative here in the colony—is that hope? Or were they just thinking it would be a way for us to be more white-passing, allowing us to avoid some of the pain they'd been subjected to? Perhaps it's ingenuity: being able to morph so quickly into someone more palatable. Black women adapt more quickly than any other creatures on earth in order to survive.

Memories and brains and myths and ghosts are all as intangible and untrustworthy as one another. We're tricked and manipulated by these things we can't even hold. Imagine my Nanny Nola storing all that pain inside her for so many decades and turning it into love for us! Alchemy. I walked around for decades not knowing that salvation from my own suffering—caused by the way my own mother parented, which was caused by the way her mother parented, which was caused by the way her mother parented and, of course, by the one before that—would come from the one woman who was the closest to it all, and that I'd be completely blind to the way those myths and ghosts travelled through time right up until Nanny Nola revealed her hand in her final moments.

Trying to ignore the impact of trauma on your life is like trying to put your hands through a rose bush without scratching your wrists. You writhe and contort and manoeuvre to try to avoid breaking the skin and drawing blood, but it happens anyway, and you end up so sore and busted up from trying to avoid the thorns that it's impossible to know what hurts more: the wound, or trying to avoid it.

Sometimes you come out the other side battered and

bruised, but it's the only way you know how to exist. Sometimes it can prevent you from being the kind of mother you'd hoped you would be.

We can overcome poverty and be 'upwardly mobile', as they say, but the ghosts never stop haunting us. They make themselves known in the throes of panic about some broader, unrelated conflict. Or more specific but irrational Aboriginal trauma manifestation.

'They'll take my kids away.'

'What if someone finds out I got too drunk or that my husband smokes pot at his friend's house?'

'They'll send someone for my baby.'

These are things the black mothers in my life have said to me. I've never had a white girlfriend speak like that, even though they do all the same things. Sometimes they do even worse. This week I read about a woman in America who had the gall to call herself a mummy blogger and was later accused of abusing her kids.

The sad thing is, I don't think the fear in black mothers is misplaced or irrational. They're right to be scared.

This fear is why my grandmother had the whitest whites hanging on her clothesline, the cleanest floors and the most rules. When she started having fair-skinned children, she was terrified they'd be taken. My sister and my friends who are mothers share the same fear. It's why when we were growing up, we knew that to be considered equal we had to be better at everything. Flawless.

This fear, these expectations are embedded in us now. It's in the Uluru Statement from the Heart: 'Our children are aliened from their families at unprecedented rates. This cannot be because we have no love for them.'

It's not because we have no love for them. It's because we've been taught to have no love for ourselves.

I have a childhood memory of hearing someone say that black women like being beaten. From that young age, I was taught that my mum's life was worth less, and therefore so was mine.

I wrote about this topic for *The Sydney Morning Herald* in 2018:

> A woman only 33 years old, lying naked, bruised and bleeding from her vagina, was found on a beach on the north coast of NSW.
>
> Dying, probably over hours, from internal injuries sustained from what her rapists called a 'wild sex' party. She had seven children who have been left motherless.
>
> It wasn't widely reported at the time. In 2016 the ABC program *Four Corners* did a story on her because at that

stage no one had even been charged.* There were two men with her when she died, covered in her blood, and recorded having panicked conversations, but they weren't charged, and they still hadn't been when the program went to air—five years on from the horrific event.

The woman's name is Lynette Daley. Have you heard it before? I don't blame you if you haven't.

She was Aboriginal.

As Aboriginal women, our lives are worth less than other women's lives.

We know that. We live that.

Under the eyes of law, as reported by the media and even by the judgement of the general public.

If that was a non-Indigenous woman people would be marching in the street—demanding changes to laws and questioning why two men with previous assault charges and who make no contribution to society could get away with not having been charged for so long.

If you tell a mother that she's worth so little, how on earth is she supposed to mother properly? If her own mother could barely scrape through the trauma of existing, struggling to show

---

* After the *Four Corners'* story, 'Callous Disregard,' aired, the two men were charged and eventually found guilty in 2017.

her child any love, then how is she supposed to know how to love her own children?

In *Sisters of the Yam: Black Women and Self-Recovery,* black feminist author bell hooks describes how, when you're black, love is an act of defiance. I've come to realise that as a black woman, showing happiness, and particularly sweetness, is resistance. I've seen the women in my lineage robbed of the right to be soft and sweet and to feel however they feel without being described as weak or angry. They were forced to be staunch lest they be walked all over.

I refuse to let anyone take my sweetness from me and force me into a way of being that's unnatural. In a world that is so cruel towards black women, to simply exist as we are is an act of resistance.

My earliest memory of my mum is listening to her laugh reverberate through her chest as she cradled me on her lap and talked to other adults at a barbecue. Or it's pretending to be asleep on the lounge or in the car at the end of a long trip so she'd have to carry me to bed.

At some point, my mum's sweetness, and her ability to direct it towards her children, faded. I remember her screaming down the phone one day when my stepdad was in jail, and when he asked her what happened to the lovely girl he'd met, she said that he'd killed her. I think that's true. He beat and berated the sweetness out of her and made her harder than she was ever supposed to be.

My mum tried so hard, but how far can you go when the only man you've ever loved forces you to finish cooking his dinner after your waters have broken, ready to give birth to one of his children? Realistically, how can you mother when so much of your energy is swallowed up just trying to survive?

The same Arundhati Roy quote I mentioned earlier comes to mind: 'Need was a warehouse that could accommodate a considerable amount of cruelty.'

My mum drove around in an old car to pick us up and drop us off. It made a noise like a siren of some sort but even worse, because the screeching was inconsistent and at a pitch that made it sound like an air raid was about to bear down on us. You could hear the fan belt from the other side of town. The brakes were just as bad. The whole thing was a metaphor for our lives: barely running and held together with rubber bands and sticky tape.

Now, when I think back to those times, I think more about the sacrifices our mums make to get us through life. Eating last or not at all. Sleeping less to get school clothes ready or prep lunches. Cleaning up, encouraging schoolwork, supporting a moody teenager, smiling proudly at a young woman. These beautiful, and sometimes difficult, moments require constant strength and an energy that is both physically and emotionally exhausting.

My friend once told me that mothers are only ever as happy as their saddest child, and I know that must be true because that's how I feel about my little brothers and sisters. Sometimes it's a curse to love people that much. Their pain isn't halved when it's shared—it ends up doubled or quadrupled, because you want nothing more than to ease their suffering that you end up carrying the weight of it yourself.

That's why our mums get in such a flap over Christmas dinner, wanting everything to be perfect, and it's why they fuss over details the rest of us can barely lift our heads to take note of. That's why they want us to come home and never leave.

———

In another hour, on another day, this one deep in Sydney's Eastern Suburbs, I was doing a Bonds campaign with my mum for Mother's Day. Much to my surprise, it was there at a commercial shoot that I found liberation from the shackles of resentment I'd been harbouring for decades. As we sat on a couch on a film set in a fancy house in Dover Hill, decked out in comfy Bonds clothes, the crew quizzed us on what we remembered from my childhood and what I'd learned from my mother. It was hardly the setting to divulge the most tender or painful recollections, but we indulged them.

'When we were little, I remember we didn't have very much, but Mum would always look after people in our neighbourhood or from school,' I told them. 'And I think that's something that has really stuck with me, not just in my career, but in my personal life as well: to always look after other people.'

My mum was quick to follow: 'Brooke was always very determined, very strong, very opinionated. I always knew she was going to be something special. I used to say you can be anything you want to be, it doesn't matter what anybody else says. You can be whatever you want to be. You can't not be proud of her. She's amazing. She's just a beautiful girl.'

I'm not sure that, when written on a page, these words can convey what was happening in that moment. For a split second, I was provided a window into my mum's thinking. She had always had tenderness and hope for me and my siblings, and because of our innate strength, she somehow knew we would be okay. She had always seen us, but she couldn't soften and show us until much later, when it was safe for her to do so. If she softened, she might've been trampled and then who would protect us?

The trauma left behind by these ghosts is our inheritance. Our birthright is trauma and pain and, if we're lucky, overcoming or defying the odds.

Governments can't send out hungry ghosts to chase kids and turn their parents into shadows without it leaving scars. Some things, once they're done, they can't be undone. Even if we refuse to talk about it for years and years, the legacy lives on in all of us. You can't take children away and then say sorry to their descendants 70 years later and expect it to be okay. If you show people what lovelessness looks like, they can't forget that it exists.

No one has said it better than the inimitable Paul Keating, when, in 1992, as prime minister, he delivered his 'Redfern' speech:

> . . . It was we who did the dispossessing.
>
> We took the traditional lands and smashed the traditional way of life.
>
> We brought the diseases. The alcohol.
>
> We committed the murders.
>
> We took the children from their mothers.
>
> We practised discrimination and exclusion.

It was our ignorance and our prejudice.

And our failure to imagine these things being done to us.

Our oppression didn't just occur as a matter of circumstance: it was deliberate and violent. It was orchestrated at the highest levels of government and experienced in the dirt on the outskirts of town.

What a privilege it would be to only have to imagine ghosts and not experience them every day.

3.

Endurance

On Australia's toxic love of sport

'Beauty is not the goal of competitive sports, but high-level sports are a prime venue for the expression of human beauty. The relation is roughly that of courage to war.'

David Foster Wallace, *The New York Times*

When I'm home alone I watch football, and it makes me feel like I'm a part of something. When I'm there in person, I can hardly imagine anything more exhilarating than seeing my team come from behind and win in the dying minutes of the final quarter. This feat unites us all in our pain and glory. We taunt and jeer and cheer and applaud in equal measure. We can experience the full range of human emotion in just a few hours.

During the winter months, when there's Thursday night footy on free-to-air TV, I find peak contentment in ordering two small pizzas—one Hawaiian and one pepperoni—a garlic bread and a can of Coke, then finding a comfortable position on the couch and watching the game in solitude. There is no greater measure of my hard work and success than being able to do this for myself. I don't want company; I don't want attention. I want to watch football and eat pizza in peace.

I've been told that people judge you by which college you attend at Oxford, and I think the same can be said for the football team you support. If you cheer for the Sydney Swans or Melbourne Demons, you're posh or a snob. In the NRL, if you go for a team that always loses, it shows people that you're loyal and think of yourself as something of an underdog. Our allegiance to our team shapes us and lets other people know how we want to be classified.

For black people, sport gives us a sense of pride. It's something we're not just good at—we're the best. In a country that prides itself on telling us all the ways we fall short, there's nothing better than seeing the young men and women in perfect form who run out and represent us.

To answer why black people love sport so much is to ask a much bigger and broader question about our society. We are obsessed with it. It's not just a distraction from the monotony of life, it makes life richer. It's impossible to overstate how much pride and passion it evokes—akin to a religious experience or some kind of graduation. When you do understand it, it's like looking at a magic eye picture and having it eventually come into focus. Our contributions, indisputably marked by tallies of goals, tackles and metres gained, are deeply intertwined with how high we hold our heads. That's why we love sport: it's where we defy the odds. It's the one part of society where our compatriots are forced to cheer for us and want to see us win.

But as much as they might want to see us win, when those same sports stars step out of line, they're instantly punished and scorned. Endless talkback hours and column inches are devoted to their weaknesses and laziness. *We* might love watching them being built up with lore and myth around their feats of strength, but *they* love tearing them down.

But politics and outrage aside, I am a huge sports fan. And mind you, it's not just football that makes me feel alive.

I love Test cricket, not least because it runs for five days. It is a uniquely Australian experience to be able to potter about the house making sandwiches out of leftover Christmas ham and ducking down to the beach for a quick swim, all while the Boxing Day Test match is taking place in the background.

But I also love it because of my admiration for things that can give me a broad and narrow perspective simultaneously. Cricket does this so well.

You've got this long game, with at least 90 overs a day, and in each of those 90 overs there are six balls bowled. So many different factors affect the bowling style and the outcome: the weather, the ball, the condition of the pitch. For example, in one over, any one of those six balls could be impacted if one side of the ball is smoother or rougher than the other, and it swings as it's bowled, or if it hits a crack in the ground in the right way. Then that one ball can impact the rest of the game. In a split second, the momentum can swing in the opposite direction and change the course of the entire Test.

To be able to simultaneously experience both the tension of a long game and the excitement of every ball is actually quite magical. It's lovely to witness all the anticipation and the expectations and then, if you're lucky, a result. To me, that part of watching sport is poetry.

Do you remember the TikTok trend last year where women would ask their partners or dads how often they thought of the Roman Empire, and it turned out it was way more frequent than anyone had anticipated? And then it spawned a way of speaking where people would say, 'my Roman Empire is . . . [insert niche subject here]'?

Well, my Roman Empire is actually the Roman Empire.

I went to Rome for the first time last year, and there are statues of Romulus and Remus everywhere. The statues are quite graphic, which I found both a bit interesting and a bit horny. It also made me think about the Colosseum a lot. Did you know that one time they filled it with water to re-enact a naval battle, but nobody can figure out how they got enough water in or out of there for the boats to float? Fascinating stuff.

The Colosseum is, of course, most well known for the epic battles between gladiators or slaves and wild animals that took place within its walls. One hundred thousand people would cheer from the stands while slaves and prisoners were torn limb from limb.

That's the same number of people who pack into the MCG on a warm September afternoon to watch dozens of young men risk their health and wellbeing to bring us joy and unite us behind a team or club. We scream their names; we chant for our club to run over the top of its enemies; we stand to attention and jump and yell in ecstasy or agony when the play reaches a crescendo and the blood of our heroes is spilled. We want rough play, and we want fierce competition. We want entertainment.

There is a gladiatorial aspect to sport in a modern context that we don't always fully acknowledge. When we watch documentaries or visit Rome, we like to think that we're so much more advanced than a society that watched slaves butcher each other or fight animals. But we're really not. We are fully capable of condemning athletes to a bleak future without interrogating what led them there, and though we are quickly becoming aware of the long-term damage wrought by fierce and violent competition, the policies protecting athletes haven't progressed at the same pace. Sometimes they even seem to be at odds with the evidence offered up by modern science.

I watch a lot of football, and I read a lot of commentary about football and other sports. I've spent more than my fair share of time in stadiums watching these men and women perform stunts that should be impossible. But I'm growing increasingly uncomfortable at the potentially lifelong injuries they incur for the sake of my entertainment.

I watched a game of football this week where one man stood in position, singularly focused on taking possession of a ball hurtling through the air towards him, while a player from the opposing side ran towards that same ball at full speed. At the last minute, the running player glanced in the direction of his opponent, and with the full weight of his body and the inertia of his run-up, his shoulder struck the man's head and knocked him to the ground. His neck was momentarily stretched between his body and head, which were forced in different directions as he hit the grass. His arms went stiff, and he laid on the field motionless for a moment or two.

There was another incident last year that drew widespread condemnation and a $100,000 fine. Two players from Port Adelaide Power ran towards each other with the same strength and ferocity I described above, and despite both men showing the immediate hallmarks of concussion in the aftermath of the clash—loss of consciousness, stiff arms—they were cleared by the team doctor to continue playing. At the time, the coach of the team, Ken Hinkley, defended the decision to send the men back on field to play the rest of the game: 'I was absolutely surprised myself how clear he looked and how bright he looked. I don't think Aliir had an issue himself . . . Lachie didn't fail a concussion test . . . he was subbed out with a migraine. He'd done the concussion test and he passed.'

I'm impressed by these two athletes and their acts of valour and athleticism, but I'm also worried about what's at stake when I see head knocks of this kind, particularly because it happens so often.

Boston University says it's the repetitive nature of these injuries that is concerning: 'We believe CTE [chronic traumatic encephalopathy] is caused by repetitive brain trauma. This trauma includes both concussions that cause symptoms and subconcussive hits to the head that cause no symptoms. At this time the number or type of hits to the head needed to trigger degenerative changes of the brain is unknown.'

But the sense of ambiguity means guidelines about head injuries in sport are still being drawn up.

It's all a world away from how drugs in sport are spoken about. Former Olympic champion swimmer, James Magnussen, made global headlines after saying he'd 'juice to the gills' and try to break the world record for the event he's most famous for. It's for a contest called the Enhanced Games, where athletes will be paid astronomical amounts of money to see how far they can push their bodies aided by performance-enhancing drugs. He was widely condemned for his comments.

There are obvious arguments about the classification of some drugs as performance enhancing, like human growth hormones, while others are classified as medically necessary, like cortisone, even though the latter allows athletes to persevere through pain which would otherwise rule them out of contests. The discussion that seems to be overlooked is that one of the main reasons steroids, or human growth hormones, are banned is because of the damage they cause, like early heart attacks, tumours and psychiatric problems.

To this point, CTE also causes severe psychiatric problems. It's a condition characterised by nerve damage within the brain, and in reality it looks a lot like early-onset dementia. Sufferers can experience outbursts of anger, proclivity to dangerous or impulsive behaviour, addiction, and a higher likelihood of suicide. Unfortunately, it can only be properly diagnosed once the person is deceased and an autopsy is carried out on the brain.

Boston University leads the research in CTE. In one study, they found the condition in 99 per cent of the brains of former NFL players they examined. That's 345 of the 376 brains that were donated. The study triggered a huge response from both the NFL and the broader sporting community. Although the league was initially reluctant to address the problem, they've since settled a multibillion-dollar class action and are now introducing preventative measures to protect players.

The AFL is about to have a similar come-to-Jesus moment as a class action begins here. The lawsuit in Australia claims the league has known about the long-term impacts of repeated head knocks on players for decades.

The Guardian reports the claimants are saying the league hasn't done enough to protect players: "'The claim alleges that the AFL was aware of the substantial medical and scientific evidence regarding the possible long-term effects of concussion,' Margalit principal Michel Margalit said.

"'Instead of taking steps early to protect players, the AFL dragged their feet which has left players with lifelong conditions that they will never recover from.'"

It's worth noting that there have been measures introduced in recent years to try to mitigate the impacts of concussions, like wearing padded helmets, introducing forced break periods after a significant head trauma, and applying protocols to measure the impacts of those traumas.

One strategy to address CTE is to take a baseline measurement so the league can properly diagnose when players are suffering from post-concussion syndrome. However, a friend of mine who plays sport at the highest levels told me that when players are recording their scores at the start of the season, they'll often fudge them. That way, if and when they do have a head knock, their scores will be consistent with what's been recorded at the start of the season. In other words, they'll pretend to be dopey so that when they get concussed no one will be able to tell because their baseline isn't great. It's not in the players' interests to miss games or have their value dip. Another player from a different code told me that if he was to hit his head before going to play in a significant game, he'd lie about his symptoms so he could play—especially if he was heading into contract negotiations.

When I see these athletes knocked to the ground in grotesque collisions, their limp bodies lying motionless for what feels like an eternity, and then watch them stumble around like they're drunk or drug affected, I recoil. But after they're carried off the field like wounded soldiers to a massive round of applause and play resumes, I return to hooting and hollering, trying to push my team to victory.

So while there may not be proper protections in place for athletes, there are also questions about whether the players would even adopt them. Maybe they understand the risks, or maybe they understand that becoming a professional athlete is one of a few ways to transcend class—and class and race cannot be ignored in this conversation, given the number of players from disadvantaged backgrounds who play at a professional level. The rosters of football leagues both here and overseas are stacked with players from lower socio-economic backgrounds who, without the meal ticket their athletic gifts have afforded them, might otherwise be just another blackfulla or poor kid from housing commission.

In a way, it's lovely that these young men and women are given an opportunity to overcome their circumstances, but it's a double-edged sword, because that same opportunity comes with a decent chance they'll be exposed to head trauma that could leave them with lifelong addiction and mental health issues and could lead to suicidal tendencies. It's kind of like those people who win the lottery only to end up so spoiled by their riches they fall out with their families and waste all their money. Probably better to have never known it at all.

We all cheer for our favourite sports stars when they're running down the wing to score a try, but who's there when the worst of their CTE symptoms hit and they're running from police or gambling away all their money?

Aboriginal and Torres Strait Islander people make up less than 4 per cent of the population but 12 per cent of the NRL, so we're over-represented by at least three times in the league.

It's a similar picture in the NFL in the US, where more than half of the league are black men. They might be more likely to absolutely flog their bodies and their brains to do these jobs even though, despite appearances, rugby league players don't actually get paid a huge amount of money.

The Australian Financial Review reports rugby league salaries have increased but the lowest-paid players are still only earning an average wage. While the average player's salary jumped from $358,000 to $428,000 a year, the salaries of the lowest-paid players only jumped from $80,000 to $120,000. While thinking about these figures, keep in mind that, according to the NRL themselves, a professional player will only play an average of three to four years, or 75 games.

Despite this, sport is still seen as one of the few ways that you can genuinely change your life. If you've come from nothing, there aren't many other professions where you can manifest significantly better outcomes for you and your family. The only catch is that you've got a finite window of time to bring this to fruition.

My heart breaks for these young people, because I know it's not just about the money—it's also a way to prove your worth and to make your family proud. Who wouldn't want to be showered with accolades and reverence instead of shame and misery?

Endurance

Mind you, these aren't always mutually exclusive experiences.

While black athletes are winning flags or scoring goals, they're considered 'one of the good ones'—but what happens when they speak up?

In 1997, Adam Goodes, an Adnyamathanha man who grew up with his mother, herself a child of the Stolen Generations, was drafted to the AFL at pick 43. He went on to become a dual Brownlow Medallist (our version of the MVP), a dual Premiership player and a four-time All-Australian. There's hardly a more decorated player in the history of the game, but it's not just his skill or ability that people will remember him for in the decades to come.

At the peak of his career, Goodes called out an experience of racism while he was on the field. Shock jocks and breakfast hosts revelled in the opportunity to blame him for what had transpired rather than point the finger at themselves or their game. Goodes handled the situation with unparalleled dignity. The crowds booed, but he dug deep and continued to perform at the highest level. He became an anti-racism campaigner and was named Australian of the Year for his efforts off the field.

Years later, I interviewed Goodes for *GQ* and asked him whether he regretted anything. I was thinking about how much pain he'd endured and how his career prematurely ended in a manner that didn't fit the script, especially given how the early parts of his career unfolded. Because of that pain, I thought he might have had a skerrick of regret, not for having done the right thing, but maybe that he didn't avoid some of the suffering he went through.

As always, Goodes surprised me:

You know, people say, 'well, if you didn't call that girl out, do you think all this might not have happened?' and I say, 'well, I did call her out, it did happen' and to be honest, if I didn't call her out the likelihood was I wouldn't have been nominated for Australian of the Year, let alone win it. Then I wouldn't have met my partner, now wife and mother of my child, Natalie, during that process. So, at the very least of it all, when I look back, I met my wife and have my beautiful daughter here with me today.

In all likelihood, even without the disruption of that particular incident and the chain of events it set in motion, there probably would have been another racist incident within the AFL. As soon as players are perceived to be too big for their boots, Australians tend to want to remind them that they're being paid to play football and not to tell them how to live—or more specifically, not to tell them to stop being racist.

It's a well-trodden trajectory: athletes realise their power and start to be seen as role models, so they speak up about what's important to them. This kind of advocacy can be extremely effective; we see sports diplomacy deployed as a public relations strategy quite often. We idolise these players on the field, so it's not a stretch for them to leverage some of that goodwill to try to make us all more thoughtful and generous people.

At some point, these athletes realise their good fortune is likely due to a combination of good genes and an ability to persevere both the most rigorous training regimes and the most intense games. They are also faced with constant reminders about how that good fortune and their work sets them on a dramatically different path than people who have miserable luck, lead difficult lives and, unfortunately, can't catch a football. They travel out to communities or visit jails and see what could've been. Like me, when they visit those places, they might think, *there but for the grace of God go I*. If our cards had been dealt differently, then our lives could have easily been swapped.

It's not a situation unique to the Australian context—look at the response to Colin Kaepernick taking a knee in 2016, or at the African American Olympians raising their fists in protest during the national anthem at the Mexico City Olympics in 1968. If these kinds of actions are about drawing a line in the sand and drawing attention to an issue, then you'd have to argue that they are pretty effective.

On this continent, Adam Goodes isn't the only one to have had his career end prematurely because of racism. Cyril Rioli was one of the most gifted AFL players ever to take to the field. His feats were awe-inspiring. Those who know the game well know just how incredible he was as an athlete. Josh Gabelich from Fox Sports wrote a gushing tribute listing his rare talents:

- Never has a player needed so few touches to have such an enormous impact.
- The stats that didn't count. The deft tap on or paddle along the ground.
- The chase down tackles that turned a game on its head.
- The creation of defensive pressure for small forwards. Did it even exist before him?
- The adoration from Bruce McAvaney that allowed 'delicious' and 'special' to become part of the footy vernacular.
- His ability to collect the ball at full pace with opponents on his hammer, gather and goal or hit the target.
- That phenomenal lateral movement.
- His humble nature, despite being so freakishly talented.

Endurance

But at the height of his football career, Rioli walked away from the game. There were allegations of racism at his club, Hawthorn, the most egregious of which have been denied by those involved:

> In an interview with *The Age*, former Hawthorn football club welfare manager Jason Burt—one of three men at the centre of allegations made in the Hawthorn review—said he would not be apologising to former players and their partners but admitted he regretted an incident in which he accompanied [two coaches] to the home of 'Zac' and 'Kylie', a First Nations player and his pregnant fiancé.
>
> Burt told *The Age* the latter incident 'overstepped the mark from being supportive to what could be deemed intimidating . . . I get that and that's what makes me feel uncomfortable.'
>
> Burt claimed he was not present for a meeting in which 'Ian', another former Hawthorn player interviewed for the Hawthorn review, has alleged he was told by [a coach] to have his partner's pregnancy terminated for the sake of his career.

These allegations went much further than the treatment or mistreatment of players, with the harm extending to the players' families. As mentioned above, one of the stories that came out was about a young Aboriginal woman being coerced into terminating a pregnancy. I wrote about this allegation in *The Sydney Morning Herald* at the time of the report's publication:

> I'm not going to talk about the fact that a 28-year-old man from this club walked away at the peak of his career and we were all led to believe that it was some sort of force incomprehensible to the rest of us—a mystical walkabout, a familial pull that dragged him away from prosperity and success and not deeply entrenched racism.
>
> I'm not going to talk about the fact that the club president, at times, carried around a golliwog dressed in the team colours and 'affectionately' called it Buddy after Lance Franklin.
>
> I'm not even going to talk about the fact that just a couple of months ago, out of Adelaide, there were accusations of some kind of Denzel Washington *Training Day*-style camp complete with men dressed in paramilitary gear armed with fake guns.
>
> What I'm concerned about, like many others, is that this is not a one-off occurrence. That this is the beginning of an incredibly difficult conversation about how we treat these men behind closed doors before we expect them

to go out and perform for us on the field, win us flags, sponsors, and members. I'm terrified that this game I love and speak so proudly about is harbouring something I'd be ashamed of.

In an unenviable position, the AFL's General Manager of Inclusion and Social Policy, Tanya Hosch, said it best: 'I think the country has a problem.'

I must stress that most of what was published in the Hawthorn report was denied by those involved, and a probe later carried out by a panel of investigators at the AFL made no findings. However, the club and former players later settled after mediation talks. Hawthorn paid a settlement to the former players, led by Cyril Rioli, but reached it without coming to a determination over the allegations. They released this statement:

> Hawthorn accepts that the allegations were made in good faith, and has heard, respects, and accepts that they represent their truths . . .
> Hawthorn is sorry and apologises that the former players, partners, and their families, in either pursuing a football career, or in supporting such a person, experienced ongoing hurt and distress in their time at the Club.

Players like Goodes and Rioli are damned if they do and damned if they don't. On the one hand, if they speak up and say that this kind of racism isn't acceptable and needs to be stamped out, they are booed and mocked relentlessly. On the other hand, if they stay silent, their careers are cut short anyway because of how painful it is to suffer in isolation.

Have you noticed how the main difference between popular Aboriginal performers and those who receive harsher criticism is that the former don't really focus on their Aboriginality or raise uncomfortable issues? Being unashamedly black is met punitively by mainstream audiences. Mainstream audiences are happy to celebrate them until they are made to feel uncomfortable or are reminded of the privilege one group has over another, while there are also excuses offered up for the poor behaviour of men and women who aren't black. There are different standards of behaviour for people of colour in public arenas, and these standards are impossible to manage or keep up with because they constantly shift and evolve. Trying to meet these expectations is an impossible and futile task.

Take, for example, Ben Cousins, the former West Coast Eagles star who in 2024 was a contestant on *Dancing with the Stars*. He had numerous run-ins with the law, was accused of taking and abusing both recreational and prescription drugs, and allegedly evaded police in an attempt not to be breath tested. And yet last year he was given a job as a presenter on one of the biggest TV networks in the country. I can't imagine the same kind of generosity and forgiveness being extended to a non-white player. Can you imagine the uproar if Adam Goodes had a rap sheet like that?

There's a thinly veiled disdain towards Aboriginal people in this country that can only be the result of a deep discomfort with exploring the truth about our past. Why is it considered so offensive or repulsive to hear about what has happened here, or to hear Aboriginal people advocate for those who are less fortunate? There's no logical explanation for the kind of wilful ignorance that happens on this continent.

The year the Hawthorn racism allegations were aired, I felt conflicted about going to the AFL grand final. By participating in an economy that allegedly allowed those Hawthorn players to be treated so appallingly, it felt like I was betraying those same young men. I champion the AFL at every opportunity. I spend my money, and I take their money. I defend it! And for what?

It's a deeply uncomfortable inquiry: am I being hypocritical?

At this particular juncture in history, sport does something for many of us that no other club or religion can do. It makes us feel like we belong to something bigger, and if channelled correctly, that feeling can have positive impacts on social issues. For example, take my football club: the Sydney Swans. One of the reasons I feel so proud to be a part of the club is because they were the first AFL team to take part in the AFL Pride Round in support of LGBTQIA+ rights. They play a major role in the AFL Indigenous Round, where they play for the honour of taking home the Marn Grook trophy.

Marn Grook is the name of a game played by Aboriginal people. The traditional game was played with a ball about the size of an orange and made from possum skin, which was filled with pounded charcoal or grass. The ball was then bound using kangaroo sinews, and two teams of up to 50 players each then kicked and tossed it around.

Adam Goodes wrote about the link between Marn Grook and AFL in *The Australian Game of Football: Since 1858*, edited by Geoff Slattery:

> I do know we were playing a similar game for the joy and excitement of it, before the said founders of the game, Tom Wills and James Thompson and William Hammersley and Thomas Smith, came along.
>
> I don't know the truth, but I believe in the connection. Because I know that when Aborigines play Australian Football with a clear mind and total focus, we are born to play it.

Endurance

Being part of the collective experience of being at a sporting match can be quite powerful. Those who love and follow sport will know full well what I mean.

I went to London in December. While I was there, I watched a Tottenham game, because their new team manager, Ange Postecoglou, happens to be Australian. It was one of the most incredible sporting experiences I've ever had, and I've been to grand finals in both codes and attended tennis matches at the Australian Open. To see all these English men, who are famously quite unemotional, weeping in the crowd and singing songs together was like a religious experience. There is no other forum for adults, particularly men, to communicate their feelings so openly. At a sporting match, you can cry or scream out of rage or laugh with delight. It is a place of unbridled joy and sadness. There's really nothing else like it.

David Foster Wallace does a nearly perfect job of explaining what it's like to love sport. In his writing, he describes in intimate detail the style in which each tennis player moves around the court and approaches the ball, causing it to strike certain parts of the racquet and then the court at specific angles. All the while, Wallace puts those small movements into the greater context of a broadcast televised to millions around the world, and he even goes as far to explain why those broadcasts differ from country to country. He somehow manages to describe the minutiae of sport without losing sight, quite literally, of the broader picture and context. This is what sport does: it neatly packages both the micro and the macro in a single experience. You can see both the broad and fine brushstrokes as though they're being painted simultaneously. Expanse, wonder and innovation exist within the rigidity of rules designed hundreds of years ago.

Within those confines, athletes and experts continue to push the envelope in the exploration of the limits of the human form. Think about it: all the people who are on the pitch at any one time in any one sport are the best in their field. They're the strongest and the fittest, and they're all training as hard as each other; if they're on the same team, they're following the same exercise and recovery routine. So, when it comes to a grand final or the final day of a Test, or whatever the pinnacle of their particular sport might be, and the game is hanging in the balance, then it all comes down to their grit and determination. The idea that a sportsperson can find an extra something within themselves and perform a tiny bit better than their competitors, showing us a little bit of magic, is incomprehensible to me. They technically have the same capability as the rest of the athletes, but for some reason on that day they had a stronger mental fortitude or were able to tell themselves a story that let them access another gear.

Endurance

As a society, we are obsessed with sport. Not just the games or the players themselves, but also the machines that surround them. In the United States, direct earnings to the NFL amount to more than $20 billion USD a year, and that doesn't take into account the contributions to the broader economy from merchandise, gambling, tourism or ticket sales. In Australia, the sports industry is estimated to contribute more than $14 billion AUD annually to overall gross domestic profit.

The influence of sport on culture is immeasurable. Over the last few years, the most talked about popular documentaries and TV shows have centred around the lives of athletes and sporting clubs. The route that players take from the bus through underground tunnels into their change rooms has turned into a fashion parade, with players styled as if they're about to walk on a runway, not go out and play football.

Everywhere you look, you can see the influence of sport. The power dynamics at play, particularly as they relate to race and class, are worth interrogating because sport permeates every aspect of our culture, both from the top down and from the bottom up.

When the football is on at Nan and Pop's house, I know I have to be quiet. I also know not to visit at all when the St George Illawarra Dragons have lost. There's a little pit deep in my stomach, close to where guilt and shame live, that is reserved solely for the feeling I get when I see the results of the Dragons' game from the weekend. I'm content if they win but a bit sorrowful if they lose. I'm not sad for the team or the players but for Pop, because I know he loves them, and I love him.

See, sport can elicit real emotion, and not just towards your team or its players, but also for the people you know and love.

This industry robs our young men and women of so much: their bodies, their brains, and sometimes their dreams. Yet, despite knowing this, I still watch. I still cheer and jeer and taunt and applaud, because while sport robs those things, it gifts us other bounties in equal measure. Sport is not just a distraction from the cruelty or dreariness of the world—it also contains moments of pure joy. And for those of us with very few options, sport gives us something to strive for. It gives us hope.

4.

The Ticking Clock

On the lies we're told about fertility

One thing they don't tell you about birthing is that it's mostly a lot of waiting. Waiting for the nurse, waiting for a heartbeat, waiting for your water to break. I'm waiting right now. My baby sister is about to have her first baby.

My baby sister is one of the sweetest people you would ever be lucky enough to meet. I remember coming back from overseas a decade ago, completely heartbroken and bereft. We were lying in bed together, watching movies, and I wanted a glass of water, so she got up and got it for me. Forget about giving you a kidney or a million dollars—having someone get up from a reclined position to get you a snack or a drink is the greatest act of service.

Anyway, I digress. Just know that she's an angel, and right now that angel is in a lot of pain.

As we're all sitting around waiting, I'm looking at the birthmark on the inside of the sole of my sister's right foot. It's a dark brown splotch, no bigger than a five-cent coin. When she was a baby, I always used to mistake it for an errant blob of poo. Now she's going to be changing her own baby's nappies and having her own memories of her baby's body that will stay with her forever. Last night, when we were sitting on the hospital bed eating pizza, I kept saying to her that it was the last night of her life where she would be alone. After today, her baby will be with her for the rest of her life, either physically or in her thoughts.

As we sit here, there are so many questions flying about and so much small talk happening. It all feels so meaningless and insignificant when I think about the fact that, by the end of the day, there'll be a new baby in our family, and we're all here to deliver it.

That's a tradition in our family. I've always thought of it as a fairly common modern cultural practice. I didn't know other women didn't have their sisters and aunties there when they gave birth until I was older. The midwife is so lovely and warm, and she is really trying hard to be familiar and accommodating, but I can't imagine going through a process of this magnitude and intensity without my sisters or my mum or my best friends by my side. If I was running a marathon, I wouldn't want a stranger running up beside me saying, 'You can do this! Keep going!'

The room is quite lovely for a birthing suite in a public hospital. There are two windows and a bench seat long enough for a partner to sleep on. There's a huge odd-shaped bathtub that is deep enough for your head to be underwater if you're sitting down. There are star-shaped fairy lights strewn across the walls and on the ceiling, and the room is painted an olive-green colour. It looks like an artist's interpretation of a birthing suite. But then there are the things that remind you that this is in fact a hospital, like the machines that measure bodily functions and dispense medicines into veins. There's also the beeping monitoring the baby's heartbeat and the beeping monitoring my sister's. Two straps are stretched around her enormous tummy to make sure they're both coping with the stress of birth.

At the same time, there are one million questions with no real answers. It's all so procedural and none of it makes sense. It's clinical and medical and doesn't at all feel like the sacred ritual that you'd imagine would be involved in bringing new life into the world.

The nurse is so lovely and chats to us between asking questions. She is telling us that it's her daughter's sixth birthday and they're going to the pub for dinner tonight.

Then the questions resume, from all directions.

'Do you feel better standing up?'

'Have you had any contractions?'

And my sister has a question of her own: 'I feel like I'm peeing, but maybe it's from my water breaking?'

I tell her it doesn't really matter if she's peeing, because everything is about to get a whole lot messier anyway.

She asks for gas, but we tell her it's too early and she should save it for when she's fully in labour. She asks for a shower, but we have to wait for the doctor to come back before she can get up.

It is exactly 10.03 a.m. Later, I will look at the timestamp on the photos on my phone and remember this exact moment.

A wave of contractions starts, coupled with intense pain.

This time, my sister stands up. 'I feel like I need to push,' she says.

Don't, we tell her. It's too early. We know that if you push too early, the cord can get wrapped around the baby's neck and make things a whole lot more complicated.

The nurse sits on the ground and gets underneath my sister to examine her, sort of like she's looking under a car. Then she says, 'Oh my god! He's coming!'

We get my sister back on the bed.

The Ticking Clock

It's too late for a shower. It's too late for gas. It's too late for an epidural. He's coming.

Now it is *definitely* time to push.

This is where the tempo shifts, and we turn into coaches to get her through this marathon. I just keep reminding her of what's at the end of this process.

'You're doing so well, my sweetheart. Your baby is going to be here in a couple of hours.'

We're not far into it when she decides she doesn't want to push anymore. She just wants him out but, as the old saying goes, the only way out is through, so she has to keep pushing.

I don't know how many babies Mum has birthed, but I've been with my other sister for two of hers. The first one happened far too quickly, and I couldn't get back to Muswellbrook before she had my nephew, Jesiah. She was only sixteen then. Now, I'm no expert, but I do think there's something about having a child when you're young that makes everything happen quicker and easier. Biologically it makes sense, I guess, even though teen motherhood is socially derided.

We're in the thick of it now, here in the birthing room. My baby sister's contractions are not far apart, and each time she has a slew of pains we know he's closer to coming out and being held in her arms.

She *really* doesn't want to push anymore; it's too painful. But it's too late to do anything else, so I say to her, 'We've only got a couple more to go and he'll be here.'

I vividly remember my other sister saying the same thing when she was giving birth the second time. She just wanted us to cut it out of her or get it out any other way. And as much as I wanted to ease her suffering, I couldn't.

'This is the worst thing I've ever done,' my baby sister groans. 'I'm never doing this again.'

I believe the first part of her statement, but I don't think the latter half is true. Not for a minute.

With each wave of her muscles contracting, she groans and we all yell things at her to help her push. In between the contractions she recovers for a little bit, still in a lot of pain, and waits for the next wave.

I take another photo on my phone, this one of Mum mopping my sister's brow with a wet washer. My sister's boyfriend is holding her hand. My other sister is at the business end of things, and I'm right in her face, talking at her.

The time is 11.16 a.m.

Another wave of contractions. Here we go.

Mum tells her she's allowed to scream if she wants to, so she does. This is how sweet she is: she had to be told she has permission to yell.

The Ticking Clock

In our own way, we each tell her to push as hard as she can—and she does. She pushes with everything she's got. I squeeze her shoulders; my other sister holds her leg up.

One huge push . . .

And he's here!

He screams. I cry. We all exhale. After all the pain and anguish of the last couple of years, he's here and he's perfect.

His time of birth is 11.18 a.m. The first thing my sister says in the video I take as he's being handed to her is, 'I can't believe I have a baby.'

My baby sister, who used to ask for Frek instead of *Shrek* when she wanted to watch it for the fifth time in a row, who gets up to make you a snack if you're hungry, who followed us around all our lives, who we used to tease by saying we found her in Japan. My baby sister now has her own baby.

All this joy after the pain of two miscarriages.

The first was harrowing. I picked her up from the train station, and we both cried the whole way home. But the second was worse. Afterwards, she went off the rails and started partying and broke up with her boyfriend.

So this whole pregnancy has been tense. Every scan, every pain, every random episode of blood spotting on her pants has felt like it meant more than it probably did.

Miscarriage is far from a unique experience, despite how isolating it is and how taboo it can be to talk about. I remember getting a call from a friend who had suffered a miscarriage at home on the toilet. She lived about 40 minutes out of town and her husband was away for work, so she had to go through the whole gory experience on her own.

Another time, I was at work as a cadet journalist, and we were stationed at the airport because of some sort of crisis that delayed all the flights. At some stage during the day, a colleague I was shadowing let slip that she'd had a miscarriage the day before. I remember her thousand-yard stare and how she seemed a bit haunted. I also remember her saying that she just had to get on with it, which is why she was at work. It seemed like a very private and personal thing to be sharing with someone so unfamiliar and so junior, but I guess I'd cottoned on to the fact something was amiss, so she felt like she needed to explain. We filed all the stories we needed to that day, and I don't think I ever worked with her again, but I do occasionally think of her and that day.

Though these stories are harrowing, it doesn't serve us to keep them to ourselves. It harks back to the days when people would keep their mental health struggles private and suffer in silence and alone. The experience of miscarriage is certainly not uncommon. When actor Anne Hathaway detailed her experience of having a miscarriage while acting as a pregnant woman for a stage production, I learnt that half of all pregnancies end in miscarriage. The emotions surrounding miscarriage are complicated, because pregnancy is so public but miscarriage is so private. As a result, the women who suffer them end up thinking their situation is embarrassing and unique. They might think, *pregnancy is a function other people's bodies can carry out, so why can't mine?* Perhaps if there was more public discussion about miscarriage, it would help ease the burden of that suffering. A problem shared is a problem halved, after all. At least for the person at the epicentre of it.

The pain of watching my sister go through that hell was only matched by the pride I felt watching her give birth. People talk a lot about the poo or the blood or the tearing involved in childbirth, but it doesn't compare to seeing someone you love do something that should be physically impossible. You see them bring life into the world from between their legs. It is magical. I wish everyone had the privilege of bearing witness to the strength of their sisters at their most primal.

While childbirth is amazing, it's also the least unique experience in the world. Every single one of us has this in common. Somewhere, at some time, our mothers gave birth to us and we took our first breath. In the same way, we all breathe in air and rely on our hearts to push blood around our bodies. We're here because someone pushed and pushed to get us here. And against all odds, mind you.

To fall pregnant is a miracle. For one healthy sperm to make it from the testes to the penis and into the fallopian tubes, swimming around to find a healthy egg at the exact moment it's ready to be fertilised, is such an onerous and unlikely task that it makes me wonder how anyone could fall pregnant at all, let alone accidentally. Then even once someone *is* pregnant, they have to grow an entire life inside of their body until that baby can cope with life outside the womb. A brain, a stomach, toenails, hair: it's all being created by their bodies. Pregnant people should be protected by some sort of iron cage so they don't fall victim to any number of catastrophic things that could happen. They could trip and fall; they could accidentally whack their pregnant stomach on something. The fact that people survive pregnancy is a wonder.

So many things could go wrong, but for us they didn't, which means we're all here and healthy enough for me to write this and for you to read it. I'm not exaggerating when I say that is a miracle.

I'm 36 while I'm writing this, and I don't have children. I've never been pregnant. In fact, I've never even come close to being pregnant. It's not because I don't have the capacity for it, which is something I had worried about. Back in 2020, I wrote about the fertility process for *Sunday Life*:

The Ticking Clock

Surely I can't be the only woman who, in the back of her mind, feels as though there's going to be punishment doled out in future for all the fun she's had.

There's got to be a price to pay for all the frivolity, the getting home when the sun comes up, for working every day for months on end, and for breaking up with men over the tiniest of flaws. In my heart of hearts, or maybe my womb of wombs, I thought the price I'd pay would be my fertility.

One thing I know for sure is that I've had seemingly endless conversations about egg freezing since I went through a breakup at the age of 33.

Even if it's not at the forefront of our minds, it's there in the background, simmering away, the ticking clock growing increasingly louder, like the tell-tale heart diorama in *The Simpsons*' take on the Edgar Allan-Poe classic.

Freedom from this biological burden used to come at the same cost as a small car but these days you can put your eggs on ice (note: this is not the actual scientific method) for the price of a flashy handbag or an overseas holiday.

Fertility expert Dr Devora Lieberman says the cost has come down because the practice has been refined using technology that has been available for nearly a decade. Costs vary but start at about $7000 for the whole process. Dr Lieberman jokingly suggests that a cycle or two of egg freezing should be included in divorce settlements for women who go through breakups in their mid-thirties.

Eggs collected from older women don't have the same levels of fertilisation success as eggs from younger women, so one of the good things about having more affordable egg freezing is that it's increasingly accessible to younger women.

For most women, the decision to freeze their eggs is not necessarily about focusing on a career, but about finding a partner they want to have children with.

It's not an insurance policy for having a baby, but it is an insurance policy against regret.

As I learnt more about my body, I felt like cracking open the champagne. I'd assumed that there would be some retribution for my lifestyle. But it turns out there wasn't for me—but it's important to get on top of it early.

There's still the stigma of being single in your thirties, with people assuming you can't find love. Instead, maybe the decision to freeze eggs should be seen through the prism of its more likely causes: prioritising career; making decisions based on values; waiting for the right person; or simply leaving options open.

The Ticking Clock

This might be the understatement of the century, but having a baby is a huge step. So I like to think of egg freezing as a baby step towards it—pun intended.

When you go in to meet with specialists to freeze your eggs, they pull out this diagram that shows you exactly how many eggs you'll need to have a good shot at a live birth, which is what they call having a baby in a clinical context. The language they use is as matter of fact as the statistics they pull from. There's no sugarcoating or baby talk at this stage of the process. There's no, 'Well, you'll have a beautiful little bubba if you've got this many frozen eggs.' It is as simple as, 'Your age is increasing and your chances of having a baby are decreasing.' The warmth and generosity of spirit you're afforded during your time with midwives and nurses in the birthing suite is notably absent at this point. I've seen the photos of babies on these specialists' walls, so I know they love and care for children, but maybe they approach it with this kind of scientific matter-of-factness because they're worried about getting your hopes up. They want to avoid disappointing their patients.

Anyway, on that diagram is one axis, which features your age, and on the other is the number of eggs you have, and in the middle is the chance you'll have a baby. It's all based on the statistics they've gathered from every other woman who's already done what you're about to do, or at least what you want to do. It's galling.

Then you wait for the results. As you wait, you ask yourself a lot of questions. Have I been kind enough to my body? Has nature been kind to me? What do I say to myself and others if there's nothing left? A million questions whirl through your head at the speed of light while you wait for the test results to deliver the answers.

Going through that process was the first time I've ever seen spelled out in black and white that declining fertility might affect my chances at becoming a mother. To be honest, as much as it was a relief to find out that I still had eggs, the whole thing did send me a bit mad.

Even still, I knew it could be worse.

One time, I met someone on a photoshoot who told me her partner had changed his mind about wanting to have children when they were in their late thirties or early forties and she was no longer able to conceive. He then left her because he didn't feel as though he'd be fulfilled in their relationship without children. It's a tale as old as time. So, like that woman begged me, I am now going to beg you, from the bottom of my heart—please take control of your own fertility. If not for the sake of becoming a parent, then at least to prevent this kind of heartache and regret playing out in your relationships.

The Ticking Clock

I'm glad I checked my ovarian reserve, because it turned out there are a lot of eggs in there. A humble-but-not-really-humble brag: when I went to freeze my eggs, they told me I had the egg count of a 23-year-old. I felt so proud that I considered adding it to my Instagram bio. I really did think I'd left it too late.

I went through the fertility process alone during one of the lockdowns in 2021. It involved injecting myself with hormones at the same time every day. For me, the most convenient time was just after I'd finished filming an episode for *Today*. I started off doing my own injections, but the needles were so unbearable and required so much energy just to psych myself up that I eventually just asked my friend and co-host Ally Langdon to do it for me.

The hormones are intense. I think it would be remiss of me not to say that. But it would be equally remiss of me not to say that I loved them.

There's a sense of guilt that comes with each part of this process. I felt guilt about having more follicles than my friends, guilt about getting a higher number of eggs retrieved, guilt about being able to afford to do it in the first place, and even guilt about undergoing the procedure at a young enough age to get a decent yield. On top of all of this, I enjoyed the hormones. I know, I'm like one of those earth mother mummy bloggers who love the feeling of being pregnant. You know the type. They probably use essential oils to clean their homes and remedy their colds.

We do love indulging in a bit of guilt and shame, don't we? I guess I'd have felt ashamed if I didn't get a result I was happy with. But it's true that the hormones made me feel like more of a woman than I ever have before. I don't even know what that sentence means, but while I was taking them, I felt like the physical embodiment of the divine feminine. I'm not sure if that's what being pregnant feels like, but if it is, I can't wait to feel like that again.

My emotions were definitely heightened. I felt everything. I saw a story about a mother and then cried for half an hour about how much they sacrifice to raise their children. This happened while we were on air. Everyone at work knew that I was injecting hormones, and they were supportive and generous towards me and my unpredictable and uncontrollable emotions. Karl and Ally both got up and did silly dances to try to make me stop crying, which of course in my state of eternal gratitude and feminine bliss only made me cry even harder.

Another time, I was driving in to have an ultrasound, which felt like such a treat because at that point in the pandemic we weren't allowed to leave our homes. The song 'thank u, next' by Ariana Grande came on, and she sang about the grief of losing her partner, then about breaking up with someone else and finally finding out that she could be self-sufficient. No shade at all towards Ariana Grande, but the lyrics are hardly Shakespeare. Despite this, the line about becoming her own best friend absolutely sent me. I bawled my eyes out in the car on the way to the clinic. In my defence, a Qantas ad on the telly had the same effect a few hours later.

One of the most profound parts of the process was being able to understand that my body is more than what it looks like. It's more than being a bit chubby or too skinny or having nice skin or hair. I had a newfound respect for how functional and capable our bodies are. I watched my body stretch quite quickly to accommodate the rapidly expanding follicles; some of them grow to a few centimetres in diameter in a matter of days. I reflected on how my genetic contribution to any babies that would be born from this batch was being cooked up at that exact moment, and I wanted to be kinder and more generous to myself to nourish their growth. I acknowledge that it was all a bit woo-woo and probably self-indulgent, but I just found the whole process fascinating and really quite empowering.

Something happens to women between the ages of 33 and 35 that means you become a bit obsessed with babies.

When I say that something happens, I mean that I went from aspiring to motherhood at some point and assuming it would probably happen for me eventually, to being distraught over the idea of it never happening for me and feeling like my life's mission was to find someone to put a baby in me. Given how quickly the panic escalated, I wonder whether the shift was due to the hormones, or if this is a common experience for women when they're confronted with the notion of declining fertility. Within a few months, I went from feeling completely content with my life to experiencing utter panic.

At that time, a few of my friends had already had babies, and even more were due. The pandemic had hit hard, bringing up feelings of unpredictability and making us all focus intently on things we could control. More than any of that though, I felt like I'd ticked off almost everything else I wanted to do and this was the next logical step. There's a common time frame for life milestones, and if you don't meet them, it feels like people start to wonder what's wrong with you. Naturally, you start to internalise part of that narrative.

I was also dating someone who, while a lovely guy, was not at all suitable for me or for fatherhood at that point in his life, but I became obsessed with the idea of having a child. I can say this now in hindsight, but if someone had said it at the time, I would have found it insulting and reductive. I started counting backwards from when I guessed I might no longer be able to bear children, and so I thought I had to find someone and settle down immediately.

The Ticking Clock

Every time someone would tell me they were pregnant or that someone had had a baby, I'd feel so happy for them, but a part of me also ached. It was a sadder feeling than yearning for a particular person or a job, because finding the right person to settle down with and love so that you can bring more love into the world is one part of life where you have very little control. You don't know when you're going to meet someone suitable. And when you do meet them, you don't know if they're going to want to have children in the next five years, let alone if they'd be a good parent.

I felt awful for feeling like this, by the way. It's so cliché for a single woman in her thirties to be a bit sad about everyone around her moving faster through those milestones of adulthood: marriage, houses and babies. I felt genuinely happy for them, but it also fed a feeling of sadness and despair that I had for myself. It's complicated to feel such intense emotions at the same time. I didn't feel jealous or any ill will towards anyone. It was all internalised. I'd have thoughts like, *when will I meet someone? When will I have a baby? What if I miss out? What if I never become a mother?*

I'd post photos of me and my family, and randoms would write comments like, 'You'll get your turn one day, Brookie.' It was all well intentioned, but I felt like I was see-through, like people could read my mind and sense my unmet desires.

I'd meditate on exactly what I wanted to do with my life. First, I'd imagine my matriculation at Oxford, and then I'd imagine holding a baby. I wanted the latter far more at that stage in my life. I've always been so maternal that having a child felt like my birthright, and if I wasn't able to fulfil it, I'd never find peace.

In the depths of this agony and self-flagellation, I had something of an epiphany. I began to reflect quite honestly about what motherhood would mean for me, and I began to feel a lot more comfortable with where I was at.

Having a child means you have less time for friends and for your career. There's no magic potion that gives you more hours in the day when you have a child. You just have to somehow squeeze more in or sacrifice some parts of yourself. You will be responsible for taking care of an entire household, not just yourself. No more long baths or saunas just because you feel like it. No more weekends away on a whim. No more gap years or fantasies of packing up and taking off. Once you're a mother, your priorities change, just as they should.

It is a sad realisation, but we must be realistic and admit that we cannot have it all. We have been sold a lie, and we must stop perpetuating it.

We also have to be unflinchingly honest with ourselves about the reality of having a baby with someone who is not suitable for us or for parenthood in general. The consequences of that arrangement are dire and lifelong. We can't appease that yearning by lying to ourselves about the situations we're in.

Half of all children born now will be raised by only one parent. So, even if you do meet someone who you think will be great to parent alongside, you've only got half a chance that you'll be able to keep doing it together until the child reaches adulthood. A more realistic, albeit far less romantic, version of the question you need to ask yourself is: Will this person be a good person to be with, and if not, will they be a good person to co-parent with if we break up?

I don't know how I got to the stage I'm at now, so I can't give you a step-by-step instruction manual for relief from the anguish that comes with realising that your body is getting older and your chances of having a baby are getting slimmer every year. What I can tell you is that for now, I don't mind what happens. I'm saying this from the bottom of my heart: for those of you yearning for a baby or a happy ending, you have to surrender to the will of the world and let whatever happens, happen. As a result of doing this, I feel happier about this subject than I have for years.

As a woman, it is inevitable that you have internalised at least some of the societal pressure when it comes to ageing and procreation. I think it's helpful to rewrite some of those stories and replace them with information that is rooted in the most accurate and recent data and, most importantly, your own values.

For example, the happiest people on the planet are single women. They live longer than men, and their lives are more fulfilling. For every person you add to your life, that happiness, according to the research, diminishes. I'm sure that is due, in some part, to the mental load and unpaid domestic duties that come with running a household. To reinforce this information and to counter the narrative that you're destined to become a chardonnay-swilling cat lady, I'd recommend rewiring some of your thinking. You don't have to subscribe to a narrative that refuses to acknowledge the full experience of women nor the sacrifices we make in order to become mothers and wives. If you like being alone or you've experienced psychological trauma that prevents you from being happy in relationships, then so be it. If you'd prefer to be partnered, that's also lovely. But word to the wise: don't just find a partner out of desperation to meet deadlines or milestones.

I would also recommend reading *Wifedom: Mrs Orwell's invisible life* by Anna Funder so you can see how we can become complicit in our own gaslighting about being able to have it all. Take heed of Funder's warning, though: 'This book is a risk: to show you the injustice of the world might harrow and harm you. Or, it might arm you against it.'

You should also read bell hooks' *The Will to Change: Men, masculinity, and love* and *All About Love: New visions*. That way, you won't end up trying to force a relationship that isn't suitable just because of some biological deadline or deep yearning to love and be loved.

There's no point lying to yourself about fertility or sticking your head in the sand, so you might as well explore your options for preserving what you have left. There are various government schemes that offset some of the cost of retrieval and storage. The cost of this process is absolutely prohibitive and, in a just world, should be covered if we want women to keep working through their most fertile years. The big tech companies now include it in salary packages for their employees. Apple and Facebook will pay up to $20,000 USD towards the process, while Google will pay for four rounds of IVF and cover egg-freezing treatments.

Though we have access to more subsidies and the technology has improved to make it easier, even taking on the burden of freezing your eggs only adds to the feeling that fertility and contraception are women's issues. You might think it is yet another example of how women are treated unfairly, but that isn't entirely accurate.

The old trope that women have to lock men down and coerce them into acts of commitment doesn't stack up. Despite the myths perpetuated in the media and even among the male cohort of childbearing age, many men also yearn to be parents. But they are even less educated than women about their declining fertility.

From what I can gather speaking to my friends, men experience different varieties of fear. Friends I've spoken to about fatherhood say they feel a unique and perhaps antiquated pressure to support their wives and children, and if they can't afford to do that, they'll delay settling down with a partner and becoming a father. Another camp is not worried at all about timing, and they find (perhaps) false comfort in knowing they can always find a younger female partner. The third group seems totally ignorant about any of the risks or potential time frames.

When we see someone like Al Pacino fathering a child at the age of 83 with his much younger, and likely much more fertile, partner, we might think that men don't fall prey to a ticking biological clock in the same way women do. But we'd be wrong.

As reported by *The Guardian*, the most recent available data suggests that male fertility, like women's, begins to wane around the age of 35. Although men don't experience it in exactly the same way as women, researchers from the University of Otago have pinpointed the 35–40 age bracket as the point at which sperm counts typically deteriorate. Children born to men aged 45 and above have a higher risk of premature birth, seizures, low birth weight, and admission to neonatal intensive care. There is also data linking an increased risk of autism for babies born to older fathers, although the evidence is not conclusive.

I hope none of this is seen as an exercise in beating up on men. I've said it before and I'll say it again: men are a mystery to me. The more I try to understand them, the more I come to realise that I never fully will.

I know that men are affected the same way women are when they're denied parenthood. They also want to be fathers and good partners, and when they can't achieve fatherhood, they are heartbroken in the same way women are. In 2023 *The New York Times* did a special report on the relatively taboo topic:

> Childlessness is now more common in men than women . . . Experts say there are many reasons—economic, societal and physical—why men who want to have children are not doing so. But there hasn't been much research on the psychological impact of not being able to become a father. The few studies that do exist suggest that the struggle to have children can have as profound an impact on men as it does on women.

I wonder what the impact would be if men came to fully realise that they didn't have as much time as they thought. Would it impact the way they behave in relationships?

One of Sydney's top fertility specialists, Dr Devora Lieberman, agrees that there are a multitude of reasons why people wait to become parents, ranging from staying at home with their parents for longer because of the housing affordability crisis to complete ambivalence about procreating. She also sent me data about men's health and how it is often the sperm that is responsible for a failed IVF cycle and infertility. Infertility is usually defined as the inability of a couple to conceive even after one year of frequent unprotected sexual intercourse. The male is solely responsible in about 20 per cent of cases and is a contributing factor in another 30 to 40 per cent of all infertility cases.

I don't mean to infantilise men, but their experience is hampered in a way that a woman's isn't. They don't have the same sort of freedom of emotional expression or open lines of communication with confidantes that we have. In an Australian context, these connections are even more constrained.

Birth rates around the world are declining, and there's something about this that feels apocalyptic and deeply sad. There are people far more intelligent and educated than me who can break down these social trends, but anecdotally it seems that people are leaving this sort of education and these uncomfortable conversations until it's too late, and then they're ending up heartbroken. Men pretend they've got the upper hand in this biological race, but all the evidence shows that's not entirely true.

There are so many things you hope for when you hold your baby nephews or nieces in your arms. I know my niece was born with every egg she'll ever produce, so for a period of time her mother housed not only her daughter in her womb but her grandchildren as well—that is, if my niece chooses to have children. I know that she will have more of a choice about fertility than the generation of women I'm a part of, not only because medical technology will continue to advance, but also hopefully because legislation will continue to accommodate the priorities of women as we're increasingly required in the workforce to support the growth of the economy. Maybe, just maybe, there'll be a moment when we can dismantle the goal of 'having it all', and the full cost of the domestic load will be exposed and evenly distributed. That way, the pressures of parenting can be factored into professional and social contributions, rather than women being left alone to languish.

Education and knowledge also drive change. These conversations simply didn't happen when I was in my twenties. Fertility was rarely spoken about; it has only recently become a mainstream topic of conversation. What's become clear to me is that fertility, bodily autonomy, and political and social contexts are all intertwined, and we must have open and honest conversations about all of these issues, as well as develop meaningful policies to support them, if we are to reverse some of the more alarming trends around parenthood and relationship fulfilment.

Despite all of this, I do believe in love, and I do hope to get married again someday and have children. But I'm not going to contort myself to fit a system that has never had my best interests in mind.

5.

Drink the Good Wine

On ageing, friendship and the passage of time

I'm obsessed with the future at the moment. I'm constantly ruminating on what my health will be like, if the climate in Sydney will continue to be unbearably humid, whether I should buy a house here, if I'll get fat, if my skin will look good as I get older, what job I might do next, if I'd be able to afford an apartment in Sydney, who will look after my mum, who will look after me, whether I'll find a suitable partner, if I should have children, if I want to have children. All of this, all the time. I feel a bit exhausted even just writing this down to be honest.

Right now, for the first time in 22 years, I'm not smoking or vaping. This is for a lot of reasons, one of them being that cigarettes smell bad to most people, and also vapes are kind of illegal now so I won't be able to get them as easily. But another reason is that I don't want to get prematurely sick and lose any of my good years for no good reason. The good years are the ones where you wake up and jump out of bed without thinking too much about where you're aching and why. You go about your days not wondering about how many days you and the people you love have left.

A couple of years ago, I was very lucky to do a bit of work that involved interviewing a lady who was about to die. She had ovarian cancer, and it seemed like she had just accepted her fate with grace and dignity. She had a warm smile that didn't betray any particular regret or sadness, and she engaged with everyone wholeheartedly and with a genuine interest in what they were saying. It seemed as though she wanted the opportunity to laugh; like a toddler who over-eggs their chuckle to delight their parents, she was eager to giggle and share moments with the women on set. There was no bitterness or sorrow or lamenting what she had missed out on or would miss out on. If that's not grace, I don't know what is.

As I worked with her, I couldn't stop studying her face for some sort of evidence of bargaining or wishing that something was different. But even though I looked at her for a really long time—maybe too much—it just wasn't there. The most special part was that she had vowed to spend the last of her days trying to save other women from a similar fate. It made me think that maybe that's what most people are searching for in life anyway: some way to help people understand themselves. Some kind of meaning.

One of the many benefits of having friends from different generations is that, if they're older, you get to reap the benefit of their wisdom, and if they're younger, you get some of their optimism. I've been interrogating if optimism and wisdom are mutually exclusive and where they'd sit as dot points on a graph with youth and experience on either axis, but I can't decide. It is harder to be more optimistic the more you learn about the worst of things. That's why practising gratitude is more important as you get older. It's easy to be grateful when you're a babe—and I mean that in the multiple senses of the word.

I do think we trade exuberance for experience as we get older. But I guess it's worth it.

Recently, I watched an old video of myself. And after reading that sentence back, I know it's self-indulgent. I sometimes say things and then regret them as soon as they come out of my mouth. Self-referencing is almost always one of those times. But no matter how embarrassing that phrase is, it happened. I watched an old video of myself. It's akin to the self-flagellating exercise of looking at photos on Instagram that you know aren't real.

Watching the video, I felt a bit of grief for having lost that version of myself. No matter how much I wanted it or how far modern medicine and cosmetic procedures and creams have come, there is no way I could be or look like that again. That little ten-second snapshot was dust in the wind. Gone forever, existing only in that place at that time.

So yes, there's no way I'll ever look like that girl again, but I'm not sure I would even want to. I know there are people who try to freeze their youth, but they always end up looking a certain kind of way, and it's not how they used to look. It's more like a new, weird version of their old self, but still not quite what might've been their older self had they just let themselves age.

I also don't even know if it was the way I *looked* in the video that made me feel like that or the way I *appeared*. I seemed kind of carefree and maybe not quite full of confidence, but full of something. Bravery, perhaps.

Am I lamenting, then, the fact that I'm not as brave as I once was? Or that I'm now more aware of the consequences of being brave so I'm more measured? Is that what wisdom is? Is it the case that I'm not jealous of my own youth but the naivety that it's intertwined with?

Youth, beauty and naivety. Time, age and wisdom. Now I know too much, and maybe I wear that on my face. I know for sure that I feel it in my aching bones when I wake up and I hear it in my thoughts before I go to sleep.

One of my wisest and most optimistic friends is Fumi Yamamoto, a person who is an expert at faces and intrinsic beauty. She also dispenses wisdom like medicine, delivering perfect phrases and anecdotes. Despite its penchant for incredible anti-ageing products, Japanese culture has a particularly useful perspective in digesting some of the more uncomfortable parts of the passing of time:

> You're moving into womanhood. There's a word in Japanese: *kao tsuki*. *Kao* is the face and *tsuki* is the intention. Your intentional being actually does show on your face. So maybe until you were 25, you would wear this face that was given, and after 25, you start to really earn how you are and how you look through your existence. So by 40, you have earned your face. When people see or feel things, it's actually not ageing—it's responsibilities. Because with ageing comes also the privilege of taking on responsibilities and, with women, the care for others. So, when we actually don't get to replenish or restore, then yes, it's on all of that level. With trauma, there's now more awareness that through the fascia, it gets trapped. We have all this tightness or heaviness. Sometimes a physical adjustment may not release it. Proper rest

and relaxation, being in alignment and feeling renewed is what will replenish you.

I guess life, you know, it's a journey. So if you have something to look back at, you can feel joyful about it, but at the same time, you can actually see that was that face, and that was one of the chapters that brought you to who you are today. It's a lovely, lovely thing to look back to.

If someone looks good for their age, does that just mean they're unaffected by the world? If someone looks bad for their age, does that mean they've seen the worst the world has to offer, and that's why they can't pretend that it's okay to prioritise sleep, facials and expensive creams?

It is a luxury to have time and money to look after yourself. It's why women who spend so much time looking after small babies go and get their hair and nails done to feel more like themselves.

I think part of Fumi's perspective is that beauty doesn't diminish with these responsibilities or the way we wear them on our faces. And the owner of one of the most famous faces in world, which has graced our screens for decades now, agreed in a recent article in *Harper's Bazaar UK*.

In the past, Kate Winslet jokingly formed the British Anti-Cosmetic Surgery League with fellow Oscar-winners

Emma Thompson and Rachel Weisz. Now, Winslet finds beauty in areas that others try to hide.

In the interview with Kimberley Bond, Winslet says that she thinks '[w]omen get more beautiful as they get older, for sure . . . our faces become more a part of who we are . . . sit better on our bone structure, they have more life, more history. Things I find incredibly beautiful are wrinkles around the eyes, the backs of hands.'

She then goes on to say:

> I've also learned it's important to take care of yourself on the inside—not just what you eat and how you look after yourself from a nutritional standpoint, but how you look after yourself from a mental wellness standpoint—how you feel about yourself emotionally, physically, how you walk through the world, how you live with integrity and sincerity.

For such a long time, we've been told that youth equals beauty, and that a lack of scars and interference—in other words, purity—is the peak in terms of aesthetic appeal. We've been told this all by magazines and television shows all our lives. It's an inescapable part of our culture.

One of my favourite people from any age bracket is my dear friend Kirstie Clements. I accidentally eulogised her once when I wrote the foreword for one of her books:

Like many of you I spent my youth devouring the glossy pages of Australian magazines. Turning the pages, carefully absorbing the messages while I sat on the floor of my bedroom in Muswellbrook in the Hunter Valley in New South Wales.

I can remember the thrill of getting home from school and seeing a new magazine sitting on my bed in the plastic sleeve. The most special of all of them: *Vogue Australia*.

So, when I stepped onto a boat at one of the most glamorous weddings I've ever been to, I was excited (although not surprised) to see none other than Kirstie Clements—one of my personal heroes. I was even more excited when Kirstie came over to me to compliment my Manolo Blahnik gold sandals and struck up a conversation. Neither of us knew many people so we spent the majority of the evening (into the early hours of the morning) in deep conversation about the state of the world and where media was headed.

I had imagined *The Devil Wears Prada*'s Miranda Priestly, but what I found was that Kirstie is one of the most inquisitive, soft and kind people I've had the pleasure of meeting. Now, she's not only a professional mentor to me but a dear friend.

I've sought her counsel through break ups, career changes and messy life stuff. I've seen her walk to the front of a line at exclusive parties and straight past the doorman before he even had a chance to check her name was on the list. I've been by her side and taken to the streets to protest sexual harassment and the treatment of women. She carries herself with the confidence of a woman who's been through everything and survived. I feel incredibly lucky to be the beneficiary of the wisdom and advice that comes with those decades of experience.

Kirstie has shaped our industry, our Australian sense of style and the way we feel about ourselves. She's a woman who's been through things. The best and the worst. The upshot of that is the insight it brings into how the world works and that you can navigate it with dignity and grace.

Both of our lives have changed a lot since her book came out. I've been through a breakup and lost both of my dogs. She's coming to terms with her own mortality as the big C spreads throughout her cohort. So, propelled by the same place that made me morbidly examine the woman's face for evidence of a struggle, I wanted to talk to Kirstie about what it felt like to get older.

I go to Kirstie's place for all kinds of reasons: because I'm bored or anxious or heartbroken or falling in love, or because I feel unmoored or directionless. The salve for all these ailments is a cup of tea and a tarot reading. Let it all out and leave it all behind.

Kirstie's home is a place of both refuge and celebration for her many friends. Its high ceilings and huge windows create space to unfurl, both physically and emotionally. And this is exactly what we did when we met to talk about ageing. That's the only clue I gave her about our conversation, by the way.

We sat down on the couch and poured some champagne, and I pressed record.

To my surprise, the first thing we started talking about was the love she has for her friends and family. Despite her background in fashion and beauty, life wasn't so much about how she and others looked anymore but how they felt. It was about longevity and health, not face lifts and skin peels. I guess I should've known that, given that she famously doesn't believe in wrinkle creams.

Kirstie: Who are you going to fool after 60? I want to look my best, but I started concentrating on being strong and healthy.

For me, it happened really suddenly. I didn't feel it at all in my fifties. Of course, I've got younger friends, I've got young sons, I'm around young people a lot, so I just didn't feel it. I'm very social and I go to parties a lot. And then I turned 60.

My friends started getting sick. And I mean majorly sick, cancers and things like that. That was a *real* brush, a real stare down at mortality and how old we are getting, even though we can all pretend we're not and we can take a nice photo and we can dress up and we can write stories about being 'fabulous over fifty'. But there are some physical realities that just hit. Then one of my best friends got cancer, *serious* cancer. Another friend has told me he has cancer, and my husband's having open heart surgery. I was talking to a friend who's in his early seventies and he said to me, it's like you have the sword of Damocles hanging over your head when you get old, because it starts to happen to everybody. It all definitely comes into play more swiftly than you think.

Without getting preachy, you've got to assess everything in your life. Wherever your priorities were, your health becomes number one. You want to be there, you want grandchildren. That's the part of your life that you want to grab onto at this age, not that you want to look like Nicole Kidman. It's that you want to be around for your grandkids, you want to be able to get off the floor without using your arms. That sort of stuff.

I think about death every day now. It's weird—I never did before. But now I just think about it all the time. But in another sense, you get to thinking, carpe diem! Where is the good champagne? Drink the good wine, see your friends, take the cruise, get married, don't get married, have a baby, don't have a baby! You just kind of grab it! Do what you want, because it's really inevitable. And it comes faster than you think.

Brooke: An aspect of all of this that I've been thinking about is that everyone is not only obsessed with youth and wellness and how we look but also biohacking and wanting to stay younger for longer. It's not just that people want to live forever; it's that they don't want to get older. I wonder if that is tied in with how we treat older people. We see that, and we don't want to be treated like that.

If you look at my friend who's Chinese, for example, he lives with his parents who are getting a bit older, and he'll be looking after them but in a way that's quite different from the way it's done in the West.

Kirstie: It's like Arab cultures. It's lovely. There's a real reverence for the experience and the contribution. It's not like, 'Oh, they're old and feeble. So stick them away somewhere and feed them some sort of slurry.' It's horrible.

I'm also seeing dementia in people around me as well. So there's this sort of forgetfulness, and if it's not full-blown dementia, it's memory. So I don't know how long you want to prolong your life if you can't remember what appointments you've got to turn up to, or even remember the fun things.

A friend of mine was just going to go and see her mother—she's 94, I think—but she doesn't remember her. Is that what's it's like at the end? You don't remember your loved ones?

The ones that, if you're lucky enough, are still around, caring for you? What's the point? What's the point of that? So medically we're keeping people alive for a really long time. But a lot of people now talk about quality of life. A lot of people think that their parents were around probably five years longer than they should have been when the parents didn't remember them anymore anyway and had no quality of life. And you feel guilty not visiting them. It's just not easy. We haven't worked that out in Western societies.

But then there's another thing too. You do wonder when you've had enough, because you get crankier and more fed up with stuff. I've been looking at the fashion shows and thinking, *god this is fucking stupid*. At what point do I check out because I don't care what you're talking about anymore? I'm out! At the moment I am in, I'm fully in, but at some point, I'll be fully out. Like, I really don't want to talk about that anymore.

The scene bores me now. Even though I bought the book. (Lol, I wrote the book!) And got the T-shirt.

You even annoy yourself as you get older. You think, *I've said that before. I've thought this before.* Sometimes I want to change my brain up.

Brooke: Is that why you need to travel?

Kirstie: Yes, that's why you've got to have new experiences. Otherwise, you just keep thinking the same thoughts.

I remember, it was probably a few years ago, I was going on a few fashion shoots, and all the people—the hair and make-up people and the models—all they talked about were new beauty treatments and new whatever: being more youthful, more beautiful, the diets, the celery juice. And I remember thinking, *it's so dull, it's so boring listening to people bang on about this*. At this point, I'm just trying not to be depressed or mad, you know? Happy and stable, healthy and reasonably upbeat. I don't care about perfection. You need to look at it positively.

Do you follow the Instagram account I showed you the other day?

Brooke: I think so.

Kirstie: I did, and then I unfollowed her because I think she's really thirsty. And I find it really disingenuous, because she keeps going on about the power and beauty of old age, but it's really that she doesn't like that she's not getting the attention she used to get from being so genetically flawless. Calm down. You had your moment in the sun.

I think it's disingenuous, banging on about the invisibility of being not even middle-aged. That's what Germaine Greer wrote books about: the invisibility of middle age. But a bit older than middle age is when you're very invisible, and with that invisibility comes great power.

People aren't looking at you as the ingenue in the room, the great beauty in the room. They're not checking out your body, because that's not the expectation. They're actually wanting to see if you're interesting, or have any charisma, or if you've got any wisdom or experience. And that's when you can really come into your power, because you're not competing with youth and beauty. You've left it behind.

I could easily walk up to any bar in Kings Cross now and have a drink by myself. And I might not have been that comfortable doing that when I was 35. (Although maybe I've always been comfortable doing that, actually.) I'm not bothered. It's something different. I'm not worried when I'm going down the street and there's a pack of boys. They're respectful because you're older. The sexual charge is taken out of it. When you take sexual charge out of it, it's really a very pleasant way to be in the world—you gain all this power.

To be honest, beauty is a bit of a curse sometimes for those who have it and then it starts fading. They're used to this elevation above others, and they want it for the rest of their lives. Certainly ageing affects them differently. It's interesting to watch actresses who have chosen not to, like Andie

MacDowell and Jodie Foster, who are beautiful. Julianne Moore's doing a sterling job of it.

Some of ageing is really good. Because you're like, oh, I actually don't give a fuck what you think. I don't give a fuck if you know my age.

Now I just don't care about the drama. People complain about things and I just think, *yeah, go do something else.* They didn't come to a party? Invite someone else. They cancelled plans? Great! Do something else.

This is where you can fall into clichés. But if you don't stop sweating the small stuff, then you'll be the annoying old lady. You'll be the crazy Karen who's screaming at people and punching cars at Walmart. But if you're just going on a sort of natural path and quiet acceptance of this march of time, then there aren't any fucks to give—unless it's about somebody's health.

This is so morbid, but there's no guarantee that any of us will make it to the end of the year. My husband might have a heart bypass and make it to 87, and I might get ovarian cancer next October. You know, it's so weird. Most likely I'll be hit by an Uber Eats courier who rides on the footpath.

Brooke: I'm in this part of my life now where I feel like an adult for the first time. I don't feel like I want to mess around with boys who are not good for me. I don't have any appetite for changing people. I know I have to buy a house in Sydney. I'm thinking about how much I actually want to work and what my life would look like if I did slow down a little bit. Also, the problems and the things that pop up that are difficult are way more serious than what they've ever been in the past. It might've been something about not getting along with this guy or my boss has been a bit short with me or whatever. Now it's more like, oh, my friend is probably an addict. Perhaps they have a personality disorder. Should I contact their family? What do we do about this?

Kirstie: I remember I had a terrible time at 54. I lost a dear friend towards the end of 2011; I lost my job in 2012 and then my mum in 2013. So in the space of two years, I lost pretty much everything. It's been okay until now, and now there are all these illnesses and seeing a friend with dementia or memory issues, another friend with cancer, and then a close family member with a mental illness.

So life gets so much harder as you get older. I don't think we thought that you have it all sorted out when you get older. To an extent you do, but then bad shit happens. It's weird. It's really weird. And it happens quite often. Somebody said to me once, your friends either get sick and die in their sixties, or they go on till they're 90. They're the two options. And it does seem to happen. That they go early or live forever.

But there is a lot of fun out there to be had. It's an amazing time to get into it. You just have to keep yourself healthy. Stay positive. You can't get to be too much of a grinch, because it's easy to get grumpy.

Brooke: Remember I told you about sitting next to that guy at the cricket?

We were having this interesting conversation about our perfect days, the best day you could imagine. I'd been for a swim at Redleaf that morning and the water was the perfect temperature, and I ordered a bacon and egg roll from the cafe and ate it on the water's edge and the yolk was runny, and then I got to go to the cricket. A perfect day! The best day! Then his friend turned around and sort of misconstrued what we were saying. He thought I was asking about the best day of his life. They were a lot older than me, and he said, 'Well, I hope it's still ahead of me.'

And I thought, *oh, wow. Yeah.* Imagine if you thought the best day of your life had already happened. I guess once you get to a certain age it becomes more likely. There are no more surprises, no more mystery. That's quite sad.

Kirstie: I think there's plenty more of those. I'm sure I thought that when I had the kids, but I'm sure I'll have that again when my grandchildren are born. Or when I was dancing on an Arctic cruise with a friend recently! So yeah, you gotta balance it out with things that are fun. But you have to have that kindness and family around you too. When you go through these heartbreaks, make sure you have a nice, soft, thoughtful group of people around you who are willing to help. Not just the party animals, but the ones who are solid.

The saddest thing would be to be lonely, wouldn't it? Or to be isolated. When I'd go to the hospital to help my friend, you'd see ladies that were doing it on their own. They were getting themselves out there and doing the cancer treatments and going home.

Brooke: I remember going to a funeral and there would have been less than twenty people there. I thought, *that's so sad*, because when you go to a black person's funeral, there's hundreds of people. At church, everyone's spilled out into the yard. Respectful, isn't it?

Kirstie: I actually don't believe in funerals. It's just not for me.

Brooke: What?

So here I was thinking I'd be having a conversation about the skin on your neck giving your age away like the rings on a tree trunk when you cut it open. Instead, when I spoke to women who've got more experience than I do, I found that as you get closer to some sort of ending, there's comfort to be found in really living. Not in looking younger or desperately clinging to the past or present. It's in accepting the futility of the struggle against the inevitable and wading through the murkiest chapters with as much grace and dignity as you can summon.

Ageing includes but is not limited to growing away from your mother as you start to unpick yourself, and the reasons why you are the way you are, and then, over time, growing back towards her when you realise the reasons why she is the way she is, and you forgive her.

It's realising that you will never love anyone or anything as much as your family, whether chosen or blood. I will never consider those who rely on me as a burden or anything other than a blessing, because to be loved by them is a privilege, and to be able to offer them the protection and security I never had is like closing a deal with the universe or fulfilling some kind of karma. It's like answering a question I asked but never found the answer to. Meeting the needs of others in ways you've been left wanting fills the void in a way that is even more fulfilling, only it's replacing the putty with gold and then massaging the surface of it with rose oil.

You only realise these things as you get older. And it does make things easier, even as the challenges you face become harder.

While I was writing this essay, I messaged the person who introduced me to the woman I mentioned at the start, the one with grace and dignity who I stared at for too long. The response upset me, even though it shouldn't have come as a surprise:

> My love,
>
> I am so sorry you didn't receive the update. I am sorry to tell you she left this world late last year after her courageous battle with ovarian cancer. She fought much longer than her doctors expected her to—and spent her final months on Earth raising awareness for such an awful disease.

This was a woman who ran and laughed and read and explored and then she died. She probably wasn't too worried about how many grey hairs she had.

There was another phrase that Fumi, the aforementioned face sculptor and dispenser of wisdom and strength, wanted to share with me during one of our precious conversations. The phrase is *ichigo ichie*, which translates roughly to 'one time, one meeting'. The philosophy of the phrase reminds us that the transient nature of experiences is what makes them so beautiful.

Our days are numbered, whether we like it or not. We only get old if we're really lucky. And whether it's the youth in a face or the fact that every time you cuddle a baby, they'll never be that small again, everything only exists for a short period of time.

As sad as that may be to come to terms with, it's a reason to celebrate every one of those beautiful experiences for what they are—especially as we age.

6.

'Natural' Beauty

On body image

One thing you need to know about me is that I will put the Paris filter on absolutely every single post I put on Instagram, and I think I'm getting away with it. I'll think to myself, *ooh, look how smooth and beautiful my skin looks. How pretty.* Then I'll click post and wait for the likes to roll in. Deep down I know I'm not fooling anyone, but I still do it every single time. It's a real elder-millennial move to think I could be swindling people with that nonsense.

There's a bikini model who I think about quite often if I'm going to the beach. She's tan and buxom, and she has long blonde hair. She's really very beautiful and has her own successful swimwear brand. Her and her gorgeous friend co-founded the brand together, and they're often seen posing for photos in exotic locations with their hair blow-dried and big sunglasses on. They epitomise what the tabloids or magazines would call having a 'beach body'. Lathered in some sort of sweet-smelling oil, drinking cold beverages and having the time of their lives. Perfect from every angle and in every light. Right?

Well. Maybe not.

I have the unusual and specific misfortune of having to trawl every news site when I get into work each day, just to make sure we haven't missed anything for the news I have to read. Today, as I scrolled through the *Daily Mail*, I saw a story about the aforementioned beach babe with a litany of pap shots of her at the beach wearing swimmers. It was right underneath a headline about a Qantas hostess stealing someone's boyfriend.

Despite not having finished a full cup of coffee, and despite my better judgement and my willingness to preserve my self-esteem, I clicked on the story. To my great surprise (and perhaps delight) she looked . . . normal.

I don't intend that to be an insult or some kind of criticism. This woman is genetically blessed by every measure, but in these photos, from those angles and in that light, she did indeed look normal. A lovely round tummy, some dimples in her legs, wet hair from taking a dip: a very beautiful but normal woman.

'Natural' Beauty

As the old saying goes, comparison is the thief of joy. But even the most wise, stable and well-rounded among us cannot help but stare at photos of people on Instagram and wonder why we don't look like that. Even if we're not wondering why we don't look like that, we're imagining what kind of rigorous workout and diet regime we'd have to undertake to even get close to it.

The feeling I would normally have after looking at images of the beach babe or someone like her is not pleasant. My immediate thought is, *I need to start doing Pilates again*, or, *I should do a juice cleanse and start eating better*, even though I know full well that I had creamed corn on toast with cheese for dinner last night. Also, I didn't have time to do Pilates today because I worked this morning and had to write all day to meet a deadline, so along with feeling guilty about having a stomach filled to the gills with food that gives me gas, I am also lying to myself about having the capacity to do something about it.

It's a vicious cycle: see a photo, feel a bit bad, move on with the rest of your day because you're busy and have a rich and fulfilling life, and then get a spare minute to look at Instagram or TikTok and start the cycle again. Despite my penchant for indulging in things that cause me a little bit of grief, namely cheese and Instagram, I am a reasonably smart woman. However, I cannot for the life of me accept that the pictures we consume of celebrities and people on the internet are probably not reflections of reality—or if they are, they're so heavily manufactured with lighting and make-up that they don't need to be retouched.

I've been in those photo shoots! I've seen dozens of celebrities in real life! I watched Angelina Jolie do her own make-up backstage at an event and then interviewed her a few minutes later. I've sat across from Margot Robbie and seen her pores before she showed me her scar from having a skin cancer cut out. I know for a fact that these celebrities aren't perfect, and I also know that I'm not either.

By the way, pour one out for anyone who's had to stand next to a retouched or old image of themselves. I've had to do it on multiple occasions. Picture me, standing in front of a heavily retouched *Today* press shot from five years ago, talking about confidence to a crowd on International Women's Day. It was like one of those old infomercials where a wrinkly woman puts some magic cream on only half her face so you could see the difference in real time. I deserve more than cupcakes and equal fucking pay with men after suffering that indignity.

The problem is that, for whatever reason, we can't fully comprehend that the images we see on our screens are not achievable because they're not real. So when we go online and see someone with no pores, a tiny waist, no cellulite, and thick, luscious hair, it makes us feel flawed or inadequate. It becomes even more dangerous when the antidote to this discomfort is either starving or modifying our bodies with medical intervention. There is no salvation in starvation.

In case you're worried, I am, for the most part, happy with how I look, and I don't have a problem with low self-esteem. Most of the time I look at myself and think, *oh, that's nice*, or, *that outfit looks good*. I don't want to look like anyone else. I'd just like to be the best version of myself, which I've come to realise is unattainable most of the time.

I'm not really sure it's worth it to be skinny all the time anyway. To be skinny, I'd have to do 20,000 steps or exercise every day, eat clean, and not go out to dinner and have a glass of wine with my friends. So if you can't go out and be seen while you're skinny, then what's the point?

A huge issue arises when people want to look completely different from how they really are. That's when they start chasing something that is not only unattainable for them but unattainable for anyone.

Early in 2024, leading news and photo agencies from around the world declared they'd issued a 'kill notice' on a photo of the Princess of Wales with her three beautiful children. The photo, published by Kensington Palace, depicted the family posing for Mother's Day after weeks of speculation about the princess's absence and the state of her health. I've talked about that at length in an earlier essay in this book, but for the purpose of this conversation, I'm interested in how easily and hastily the credibility of the image was called into question and ultimately denied.

The standard for reporting news should be high, because the news helps people to understand themselves and the world they live in. It is also a pillar of democracy; at its best it's capable of holding those with power accountable. So now that we know it is possible for news agencies to inform people when images have been altered, why doesn't it happen more often and in situations we know cause harm to vulnerable people? Given how this particular situation unfolded, we can see that there is significant power in pulling down altered images or not publishing them beyond Instagram.

If we're aware of the damage caused by the unrealistic expectations set by these images, particularly for the most impressionable among us, and if we know that so much of what we see online is manipulated to such a degree that it is not achievable without medical or surgical intervention, then why are these photos allowed to be published without any indication that they are not real? Or, dare I say it, why are they allowed to be published at all?

Social media is designed to be addictive, and we're allowing it to be placed in the hands of those whose brains are still developing. We're giving social media platforms unfettered access to the most vulnerable minds in our society and hoping they don't look at things that could have an everlasting impact on how they feel about themselves.

There is more than enough evidence to show just how harmful social media can be. In 2023, the American Psychology Association found that it's not just women and girls who are affected by this either; it impacts everyone equally. According to the research, '[t]eens and young adults who reduced their social media use by 50% for just a few weeks saw significant improvement in how they felt about both their weight and their overall appearance compared with peers who maintained consistent levels of social media use'.

Across the globe, different approaches are being taken to limit the harm caused by social media. In Florida, Governor Ron DeSantis has completely banned people under the age of thirteen from using social media, while fourteen- and fifteen-year-olds can only access these sites with parental supervision.

Despite the infinite amount of content you could consume online—the endless pictures of celebrities with perfect skin and clothes—in the end, everyone tends to look kind of the same anyway. I joked with a friend the other day about an event she had to go to, saying, 'Did everyone have that really shiny Hailey Bieber skin and an oversized blazer?' She laughed and said, 'Yep, and slicked back hair and bushy brows, and they all were wearing the Glossier perfume.'

When you read that, you know exactly who we're talking about, don't you?

Lip fillers and cheek fillers. Hollowed-out jawlines and plumped-up lips. Sydney's Eastern Suburbs is now a real-life Instagram feed. These taut, shiny images have climbed out of my phone and into my coffee line.

But even this version of natural is fake. No one wears make-up anymore, but there's so much focus on skin that children have become influencers, peddling products with acids and retinols normally reserved for someone in their late thirties. The pressure of looking 'done up' has eased, but we've doubled down on people looking good naturally, which in my opinion is much, much harder and much more expensive. It's counter-productive: we're more accepting of natural beauty, but only if you look perfect when you are au naturel. At least in the past, if you were feeling ugly you could just wear heaps of make-up. Nowadays, you can almost guess what part of town someone is from by how much eye make-up they're wearing.

One major luxury retailer reported that in 2024 young people have spent 23 per cent more on skincare, make-up and fragrance year-on-year. This is probably due in large part to what they're seeing on TikTok. The expenditure in and of itself is not really a problem, as long as they can afford it. It's that many of the products they're buying were specifically designed for ageing skin, so they contain harsh chemicals and acids designed to stave off wrinkles and things like sun damage and uneven skin tone. These products can damage young skin more than they help it. Many of them make skin ultra-sensitive to the sun and its harmful effects. On top of inappropriate information about skincare, these young people are also being fed pictures and information about fillers and Botox.

Our babies are growing up being told they need to spend money to look a certain way to be considered beautiful. But the standards are so bizarre and change so quickly that only the mega-rich and privileged can afford to keep pace.

There was a trend recently where people would post a photo of themselves and ask others to guess their age. One photo of a 22-year-old woman went viral for all the wrong reasons. Due to how aesthetic modifications had changed her face, many people guessed that this woman was in her thirties or forties.

Another instance that springs to mind is a beautiful woman who posted a picture where she wasn't wearing make-up. She said she was proud, and then she was mercilessly torn apart. One young person commented that if their skin looked like hers, they'd kill themselves. Teenage girls are prone to hyperbole, so maybe they didn't mean it literally, but the picture was lovely. The woman had a normal amount of sun damage for someone her age, or maybe even less. But because of this obsession with flawless skin, she was annihilated.

Women and girls are tearing shreds off each other on the internet—to what end? It shouldn't be considered an act of valour to present a normal, or even beautiful, naked face to the world, but here we are.

I've interviewed Lizzo many times. One time I told her that she was brave, and I praised her efforts to encourage others to love themselves. She seemed taken aback, and at the time I didn't really understand why. I thought it was a compliment.

But now I realise that no one wants to be told they're brave for loving themselves, because the subtext of that comment is that you're brave to love yourself in a climate where your very existence is political and people mock and belittle you. In spite of everything that you are, you still love yourself, and isn't that just neat? Now obviously that is not what I meant, but I can see how a comment like that would sting and not always land right.

I do still think it's brave when Lizzo unashamedly posts about herself, as she deserves to do. There are so many trolls who target her, trying to make her and others feel bad about themselves. In order to expose the world to different standards of beauty, she's making herself a lightning rod for negativity.

Part of why that bravery ought to be applauded isn't just because it's unusual to see someone who isn't thin taking up space and getting attention on the internet—it's because it draws criticism, but she does it anyway.

I look with admiration at what Lizzo's doing, but I can't imagine opening myself up to that level of criticism. Maybe it's that I know it would end up in the *Daily Mail* or some other tabloid, or maybe I just don't want to be seen. I'm happy with my body, but the thought of opening myself up to other people's idea of what's 'normal' or 'perfect' is a bridge too far for me. I don't want to be held up in comparison to other women on the internet. I don't want to hear what others think of my cellulite or boobs. I live in my body, and I can't imagine having those jibes levelled at me from anonymous profiles without it leaving a mark.

I've posted public photos in swimwear before, and within hours headlines appeared online with phrases like 'rare bikini photo'. But I also didn't have anything to prove by posting those photos. I posted them because I knew they would get attention, and I used the caption to tell people to get vaccinated so the government would ease the Covid-19 lockdown restrictions and I could go home and see my family.

No one is looking at my body and feeling inspired. It's a normal, thinnish body, and it always has been. If I'd done something or had to overcome a challenge to earn it, or even if I thought it would help others feel good about themselves, then maybe I'd be inspired to be more present in less clothing. But as it is, I'd rather not participate.

Lizzo is already liberated from the burden of being confined to a certain kind of hotness. She doesn't feel the need to appease the masses like female celebrities in the past, who needed to stay thin and young in order to stay relevant. Instead, she's created her own path. She's beautiful and big, and those aspects of her appearance not only coexist but are inseparable. Big isn't a dirty word anymore, and it's only because people like Lizzo flipped the narrative on its head.

It must make people hate her that she doesn't need their support or approval to feel like she deserves to have a rich and fulfilling life. I'm glad she's showing people that you can find peace despite how hell-bent some are to deny you the opportunity, like it's a luxury only afforded to those who can fit in a size 10.

I cannot imagine the feeling of living in your body and hating it. Is it like sleeping in a bed that's not yours and never knowing the comfort and safety of one that is?

That's not to say I haven't looked at my body and thought it could be better or fitter or more or less of something. It's just that I've never had disdain towards it because it has always, in my mind, looked relatively acceptable. Maybe others would disagree, but I don't know because I don't ask them. I've dieted and exercised excessively in the past, particularly if I had an event or a photo shoot coming up, or if I'd gone through a period where I'd put on weight and had to lose it, but it's never been for an extended period. I probably exercised too much during the Covid lockdowns, like a lot of other people. I probably ate too much while I wrote this book. But my habits normally return to a baseline.

One of the things about being on TV is that you see yourself from obscure angles every day. So if you're not happy with something, no matter how much you choose skinny mirrors or good angles, you generally can't avoid it. You also notice because you have a wardrobe of clothes in a certain size, and if you don't fit them anymore, you don't have anything to wear—and you're on TV.

I know these are far from normal or relatable experiences, but they are mine. I guess that's why I try not to let what anyone else thinks of my body change the way I view it, or at least the feelings I have towards it. It could get slightly bigger or smaller, making clothes look better or worse, but ultimately the feelings I have towards it are either that it's nice or it is what it is.

One of the (many) parts I like about being single is that I'm the only person who sees and enjoys my body. I love that feeling of it belonging only to me. I love putting moisturiser on and having a nice stretch. I wonder if the comfort I take from that sense of privacy is a reaction to being so visible in my professional life.

Going through egg freezing and fertility treatments was one of the most liberating experiences of my life in terms of how I viewed my body and the gratitude I felt for it. I saw my body as useful, and I was grateful for its health, shape and smell. All of it is glorious, and there's nothing I want other than to nourish it, and keep it strong and healthy as it carries me into old age.

I also suspect that sitting at the root of the contentment I feel about my body is intellectual superiority. I feel okay about not being the prettiest person in the room because I can also be smart and funny if I need to be. It's a level of hypocrisy that is uncomfortable to interrogate, because they're all god-given gifts. You can train, learn or interfere with nature all you want, but at the end of the day you're only building on foundations that already exist. Only for some reason there's a moral superiority that comes with being smarter than others. And I know that, to a certain extent, it's classist and ableist to value intelligence over other attributes.

Say if you did have a boring personality and you knew it, so you placed more emphasis on how you looked, like you went to the gym more and prioritised grooming. Would that then become a curse that couldn't be broken? Would you be condemned to being seen as vapid for the rest of your life because you'd rather spend your free time making yourself look good than expanding your mind by thinking or reading? The reverse could be said to be true as well. If you spend all of your time learning and writing rather than worrying about whether or not you've got a sixpack, maybe you'll never be conventionally hot.

As a woman of colour, my 'confidence' despite not being perfect may not be unique to me.

Interestingly, despite the saturation of mainstream media by white people and bodies, research from the UK-based Mental Health Foundation shows that black people have a healthier relationship with their bodies than the rest of the population:

> While the differences across ethnicities may be small, where such differences have been observed, they tend to show that, in general, Black women are more satisfied with their bodies than White women. This is mirrored in some analysis that looks at body image in Black British girls, which finds they are more likely to express a positive body image and less likely to show disordered eating behaviours than White British girls. Similarly, Black males (adult and children)

reported being more satisfied with their bodies compared to their White counterparts.

Similar research has been carried out in the United States with similar results. However, there are questions about how culturally relevant this research is given the fact that black women generally have different priorities for their bodies and appearance. I saw a quote by a black woman online that said, 'We're supposed to be thick'.

Of course, there is a danger that an increased exposure to online images of Eurocentric beauty standards will be internalised by black women, affecting their self-esteem. But it is interesting to note that many of the women I've mentioned in the essays in this book—Beyoncé, the Kardashians, Lizzo—are famous for their bodies being curvaceous or 'thicc'. When I was younger, being unhealthily thin was much more desirable—Kate Moss, Mischa Barton and Nicole Richie were the women we admired and wanted to imitate. I have no doubt the representation of racial and ethnic diversity in music and in other sectors of the arts has played a part in shifting this trend.

None of this goes any way to changing the fact that when I catch a glimpse of my reflection and I see a dimple or a round tummy, I notice it, and maybe I even recoil a little, even though I do still think I'm fine the way I am. I haven't graduated to the level of self-acceptance that Lizzo and her ilk have, where they're not only fine with what they see but they're proud of it. It still feels like I'm learning to accept something that, at least deep in my subconscious, isn't quite seen as acceptable.

I don't hold others to this same standard though. If my friend said to me, 'Oh, I don't want to come to the beach today because I feel a bit chubby,' I'd consider slapping her and telling her to pull her head in because she's beautiful and perfect the way she is. I wonder if we have these benchmarks for ourselves because of the way media used to be consumed as well. We'd devour the pages of the glossies in the privacy of our bedrooms, whereas now looking at these pictures can be more of a communal activity, where commenting and sharing plays a role in delivering content to our individual algorithms.

From what I can gather—and I don't mean to other anyone here—there are more fat people than there have ever been. The World Health Organization reports that the number is climbing and will continue to do so:

> In 2022, more than 1 billion people in the world are now living with obesity. Worldwide, obesity among adults has more than doubled since 1990, and has quadrupled among children and adolescents (5 to 19 years of age). The data also show that 43% of adults were overweight in 2022.

It shouldn't be remarkable that people get to see themselves represented in popular culture achieving extraordinary feats. There's a common argument put by those who'd like to see less representation that bigger bodies are unhealthy and shouldn't be platformed as a standard of beauty. But if that is the primary concern, then where are these voices when we see bodies that are incredibly tiny? Only this week, I saw an influencer post on Instagram their 'day on a plate', which consisted of a coffee, two boiled eggs, a Greek salad and a plate of broccoli. I'm no dietitian, but that is not enough food to sustain a busy day. I reckon I would consume more calories than that by midday.

I'm oddly and inappropriately proud when I see someone in public wearing something revealing when their body isn't perfect. I think, *oh, good for her*, even though I would never do it myself.

We have a lot of deprogramming to do when it comes to not just how we view ourselves but the standards we hold ourselves to in order to feel whole, fulfilled and at our best.

I point the blame squarely at the way young women were treated while I was growing up. I shared a harrowing clip on social media just this week in which Nicole Richie was asked whether she thought the reason she wasn't successful in acting was because she was chubby, Victoria Beckham was weighed live on air in a radio studio so they could see if she'd put on weight, and Tyra Banks tore shreds off a contestant on an old season of *America's Next Top Model*—you could read the despair on all of the contestants' tiny, impressionable faces. All these women were fine, and we were made to think they weren't. It's despicable that everyone felt they had the right to make comments about them. Millennial women bear the emotional scars of this treatment.

As I mentioned, I am an elder millennial, so I am from the generation of women who grew up on a steady diet of makeover TV shows and magazines filled with pictures of impossibly skinny pop stars and models next to articles about how we could get our dream guy (Taylor Hanson) and a beach body in ten easy steps. We internalised a standard that was always going to be impossible to meet because no one was telling the full truth about what these young girls and women endured to look the way they did. We also weren't and probably still aren't as savvy as the generation below us, who are digital natives. Maybe it is easier for them to pick out editing than it is for us, and so even though they have more access to content than we did, they're not as impressionable or naive as we are. They would definitely know that I put the Paris filter on every photo.

Being underweight and under-eating are just as, if not more, damaging to long-term health as being overweight, but because we are living in a fatphobic society, we're a lot more comfortable seeing skinny bodies than fat ones.

In Kirstie Clements' book *The Vogue Factor*, published in 2013, she describes in detail the great lengths models would go to maintain their slim physiques:

> The longer I worked with models, the more the food deprivation became obvious. Cigarettes and Diet Coke were dietary staples.
>
> Sometimes you would see the tell-tale signs of anorexia, where a girl develops a light fuzz on her face and arms as her body struggles to stay warm. I have never, ever, in all my career, heard a model say I'm hot, not even if you wrapped her in fur and put her in the middle of the Kimberley Desert.
>
> In 2004, a fashion season where the girls were expected to be particularly bone-thin, I was having lunch in New York with a top model agent who confidentially expressed her concern to me, as she did not want to be the one to expose the conspiracy. 'It's getting very serious,' she said. She lowered her tone and glanced around to see if anyone at the nearby tables could hear. 'The top casting directors are demanding that they be thinner and thinner. I've got about four girls in hospital.

'Natural' Beauty

'And a couple of the others have resorted to eating tissues. Apparently they swell up and fill your stomach.'

There's a question worth positing about the morality of the modelling industry as a whole, in terms of how and where it procures young talent. A Brazilian friend of mine who worked as a model in New York described the horrible situations where half-a-dozen teenagers from poorer countries are forced by agents to live in tiny apartments in the Big Apple so they can audition for jobs and try to make it big. They rarely do, though, and are often subjected to terrible conditions. They leave their parents and home countries to chase their dreams but, more often than not, they are exploited and left wanting.

This is yet another example of how contrived those images of models are. They're not always perched atop the deck of a super-yacht in the south of France—most of the time they're squished into bunk beds in a shitty New York apartment.

There are some people who just make you sigh because they're so beautiful. I don't just mean models, although there are some who inspire this reaction. Actors, too. Especially Sydney Sweeney.

I read an article a couple of years ago when Sweeney had just started on *Euphoria*, and she had complained that women in Hollywood don't get paid as much as they used to and so it was actually quite hard to make a living unless you're extremely successful. It was in the context of a discussion about privilege in Hollywood and how if you're not a nepo-baby, it's actually quite hard to survive. This earned the ire of pundits on the internet who slapped her down and accused her of being self-righteous and privileged.

But what she said probably is accurate. Most actors and extras don't make enough money, and Los Angeles is an expensive city. Unless they're making huge bank, they most likely don't live in a mansion or have a driver and a personal chef. They do look good, but that's because they have stylists who borrow clothes for them that are probably paid for out of the studio's marketing budget.

Since then, Sweeney has become the poster child for anti-wokeness because she embodies a beauty standard of old. And, although this is quite crass, the truth is we all can't stop staring at her tits. Boobs are objectively lovely. Even if you're not attracted to women, it's a truth universally acknowledged that you can still see a pair and think, *wow, that's a good set of boobs*. (I assume everyone thinks this way—or is this the moment I unintentionally discover I am bi?!) The argument made by right-wing internet users is that she symbolises anti-wokeness because even the most progressive among us have to admit she's beautiful, and that in essence her beauty is because of what she represents: the traditional stereotype of beauty.

But what they're failing to acknowledge is that there is now space for more than one kind of beauty. While Sweeney is having 'a moment', she's not the only one.

It's impossible to fully explain how big Sweeney's moment is. I saw a meme where someone had taken a screen grab of her eating hot wings in an interview and superimposed it on the inside of an army helmet. The caption read, 'Do it for her'—like she's at home waiting for you while you're off fighting in a war. You wish, mate.

She's doing the interviews that are quite literally the hottest thing with the most views, but I don't think all the attention is positive. In fact, there is an argument to say that her career will be hampered by her traditionally good looks. While Sarah Snook was being offered parts in TV shows that have won her multiple Emmys and performing in groundbreaking theatre productions in London and New York, Sweeney was galivanting around Sydney promoting her new movie in which she spent a considerable amount of time in a bikini or skimpy workout gear. I don't know the extent of her acting chops, but I do know that she does not have the same credibility as Snook and that her talent is not valued in the same way Snook's is. This is not her fault by any means, but—dare I say it—I think it probably will be a burden at certain junctures of her career depending on what her goals are.

It's a tale as old as time: actors who are incredibly beautiful will, at some stage, in order to be taken seriously, have to fug up. They'll have to take a role where they wear prosthetics and look fucking ugly and maybe even play someone who is a bit evil. Think Margot Robbie in *I, Tonya* or Charlize Theron in *Monster*. Robbie won the Critics' Choice Award for her performance as a figure skater from the wrong side of the tracks, while Theron took home an Oscar for her grotesque portrayal of a female serial killer.

Apparently, because Theron had to gain weight and use prosthetics for her role, producers didn't want to support the film, and right up until the eleventh hour the filmmakers were struggling to get the film distributed. In an interview with *Orange County Register*, Theron said, 'They didn't like the way I looked, and they wondered who would want to see this movie. When we finished, we couldn't pay a distributor to take it. We were hours away from signing a straight-to-video deal with Blockbuster when we found a distributor.'

While we're on the topic of Margot Robbie, there was a time when the same group that are feeling some kind of limerence towards Sweeney felt that way about our Margot. She fell victim to the same kind of projected sexualisation after her role in *The Wolf of Wall Street*, which seems like the result of men wanting to embody someone who made a lot of money and had an incredibly hot wife. There were rumours about the scene in the movie where Robbie's sitting on the floor with her legs spread, and she kicks Leonardo DiCaprio in the face. The rumours were that because her pins were so perfect, they must have been fake or a body double. It's just like how they now question whether Sweeney's breasts are implants.

The problem with this kind of projection is that it is just that: a projected fantasy. Neither of these women have any agency over how they're perceived by strangers watching their movies or looking at their photos on the internet, so when they step outside the narrow confines of these ideals—physical or ideological—they're abandoned in droves, often criticised and negged by the same cohort who only months before had adored them. For example, when Robbie created her own production company that later made *Barbie*, a film that was met with great fanfare from the feminist corners of the internet and great disdain from men's rights activists, the tide turned against her. Articles and comments about how 'mid' she is began to surface. This is a woman whose beauty is so great that she could play a living Barbie doll, and she was being insulted by trolls who claimed that she was nothing special. Average. Mid! What hope do the rest of us have if this perfect specimen is mid?

And let's not forget about the impact on young women's self-esteem when they witness a months-long, worldwide press tour, where each outfit and hair and make-up combination was more perfect than the one that preceded it, then hear that all of it was nothing but 'average'.

There's no doubt in my mind that none of this response was related to how Margot Robbie looks or even the fact that she oversaturated the market right before the SAG-AFTRA strike. It was because these men could not escape the fact that Robbie holds power, has autonomy over her career and the movies she makes, and ultimately is on her way to becoming one of the richest and most powerful people in the entertainment industry. This success is all thanks to the decisions she has made, decisions that have made it increasingly difficult for anyone to imagine her as just a submissive blonde with knockout pins. Once she shattered the illusion of their fantasy, they wanted to bring her down a peg or two.

My hope is that not only the younger generations but also us older people will one day find out what it's like to be free of those shackles.

We shouldn't take hard-won gains (pardon the pun) for granted. In an age when perfectly preened trad wives are nearly the most popular people on the internet and Ozempic is the biggest thing to come out of Denmark since Lego, we have to continue to reject the narrative that's been fed to us to make us hate ourselves so others can benefit commercially. We can't

'Natural' Beauty

let our daughters and nieces suffer in the same way we have. Everyone deserves to know what it feels like to come home to your own body and love it, not in spite of its flaws, but because of them.

7.

Indigeneity

On Indigeneity and the 2023 referendum

'I am Australian. There is no other place on earth from where I could come. Think about that: I could only have been created here. The history of this land runs through my veins. I am old and I am new. My bloodline connects me to the first footprints on this continent. Two million sunrises have put me here.'

Stan Grant

This quote is from Stan Grant's book *Australia Day,* and it is as true for you and me as it is for him. Despite how Australian I am, or any Aboriginal person is, we could not, and I fear will never, have that reflected on our nation's birth certificate.

As for the Indigeneity part of being Australian—it is as complicated as it is simple. Being able to identify where you're from in time and space and placing yourself here in Australia seems like a far easier endeavour than to define exactly what it means to be Aboriginal. We're born in this nation state that means we're Australian but, in my mind, our Indigeneity defines our character and values far more than that. It permeates every part of our identity and ways of being and expressing ourselves.

'You're too pretty to be Aboriginal.'

'Oh, but you're one of the good ones.'

If you or someone you know is Aboriginal, chances are you will have heard comments like these before. I'm making myself chuckle a little bit as I write this, because I read it in my head like one of those American compensation advertisements that pollute the airwaves of commercial TV. I guess it's even funnier because we'll never be entitled to compensation.

How would they even decide who's entitled? How do you define Indigeneity in an era when Pauline Hanson claims to be Indigenous?

Some Aboriginal people have tattoos to profess their identity, a flag brandishing their bicep or tricep or wherever it looks best or is most visible. Others might adorn their walls with dot paintings or speak in language to show their colours. It's easy to be cynical about identity politics in this climate, and I guess I am, because I don't know whether these are meaningful expressions of Indigeneity or if they're a way of performing Indigeneity for the benefit or approval of those who refuse to see you. I have a theory that these actions are fuelled more by a separation and detachment from culture than a desire for genuine self-expression.

Indigeneity

More often than not, those with the fairest skin are the ones who express themselves the most boldly. As a fair-skinned Aboriginal woman, I have a great deal of empathy for those who find themselves in a situation where their identity is constantly interrogated or denied. It is a special kind of curse to look more like the people who hate you than those who love you.

This truth is often neglected when people discuss colourism. To be clear, I'm not disputing the privilege that comes with being able to move through the world in disguise as a part of the majority. I have no doubt that my life is easier than the lives of those who are obviously or easily identifiable as black. But it's also true that when you look more black, more black people love you. When you look white, more white people love you. But what about when you're a black person who looks white? Who loves you then? That's the thing that people don't get about the privilege of being white-adjacent: you end up being loved more by the people you don't want love from. Or even worse, you're black enough to hate but not white enough to love.

It's little wonder, then, that these adornments and decorations are appealing to people who might otherwise be ethnically or racially misidentified.

I don't know whether it's common knowledge that they used to use a sliding scale of skin colours to determine who was considered salvageable and who was deemed too dark to coexist with Australian society. That is how unscientific the guidelines for removing children from their parents were. Perhaps it's also why it's so important for us to prove to others how black we are, lest we be damned to a fate that means we are banished to the margins, not just of the broader community but, more painfully, our own.

Some people look at me and immediately know I'm black because I have my grandmother's green eyes, which are very common in northern New South Wales, or because of my grandfather's last name. At least once a week, I get asked, 'Are you related to the Boneys in Brewarrina or Bourke or [insert any country town in north-west NSW here]?' So I've never really worried about whether or not other black people know I'm black. I do, however, assume white people are sceptical of me because I'm not quite identifiable as anything in particular.

If we base the definition more in the context of our cultural identity than the percentage of our Aboriginality, which, as I mentioned above, has previously been how our identity has been defined, then what does that mean for the people from the East Coast of Australia whose languages and practices were monumentally and irrevocably interrupted by the expansion of the colony? By both of these measures, it would mean we're not as Aboriginal as our brethren from the middle of the continent who didn't suffer the same cruel fate as early on. And while these

Indigeneity

measures have primarily been used by non-Aboriginal people to cast aspersions on individuals or design policies, they're also used by black people against other black people. The more closely tied or enmeshed you are with traditional cultural practices, the more 'authentic' your experience as a black person is.

Maybe Aboriginality is based in shared jokes or humour. Maybe it's in recipes or the way you celebrate certain things. Maybe it's in suffering in the same way and thinking, or knowing, that there's not enough luck to go around, so if there's anything left over after scraping the bottom of the barrel, it's not going to be doled out to you.

For many people, ideas of Indigeneity go hand-in-hand with the experience of poverty and low socio-economic status, and so these people talk about their experiences openly like they're a badge of honour or evidence of their blackness.

The term 'trauma dumping' has become common parlance as a new generation take to the internet to talk about the awful things that have happened to them. It's about extrapolating and divulging the most painful wounds in the most public places.

It reminds me of this passage from *Tomorrow, and Tomorrow, and Tomorrow* by Gabrielle Zevin:

'This generation doesn't hide anything from anyone. My class talks a lot about their traumas.'

'If their traumas are the most interesting things about them, how do they get over any of it?' Sam asked.

'I don't think they do.'

In my world, poverty isn't romantic like how some people describe it. It's not memories attached to smells and routines or biscuits and tea, like a Depression-era Australiana description. It's making do. It's a colander with a broken handle that you watch your mum use for years; it's an ironing board that doesn't open up; it's one steak knife that is used for everything. It's broken chairs. It's holes in the walls. It's full of actions that are wasteful and pointless. Like why wouldn't you just buy ten loaves of bread for $10 when you get paid so no one is ever hungry? It is poor decision-making. It's spending one day rich and six days broke. It's kids with nits in their dirty, grown-out hair.

I often think about all those kids I grew up with who had all that trauma; the lives we had then, and the lives we have now. I was thinking about the sort of things those poor, hopeless little souls needed and how people are always trying to get me to go to schools and say something to children who are going through things that I once was. Give some hope to the hopeless little souls. Tell them that I was once hungry, scared and as hopeless as they are now, but I'm not anymore. So maybe there's one thing to be hopeful about.

Indigeneity

Maybe the worst thing is not being scared that your mum will get the piss punched out of her or going to sleep with a hungry tummy; maybe it's worse not to have anything to hope for. Falling asleep crying, wondering if your hopeless little life will ever get easier. I guess mine did, so maybe that's what they want me to say to them. Cry because your situation is terrible, but don't cry, because it might not always be. Then you can worry about other things, like pigmentation or not getting invited to parties. If you're really lucky, you get to worry about your belly being so round from eating so much beautiful food on a holiday in Italy that you barely have enough time to walk far enough and make it flat again.

When I started at Channel 9, someone said to me that you should never let them see you bleed. I think that's wise advice. Why would you show people who can hurt you the ways in which you're most wounded? It's an impractical bet; you might get a bit of care, but the potential for harm is far greater.

I've never been a fan of sharing my experiences just so others will understand me more or show me more compassion. We all deserve that as the bare minimum. I'm sharing my experiences and thoughts now because I think, and I hope, it'll help others feel less alone in their feelings. I'm not interested in anyone's sympathy or support.

By the way, being poor or having trauma isn't specifically what Aboriginality is either. Though there are very distinct ways of being poor when you are Aboriginal.

Is Aboriginality found in mattresses dragged into the living room, or in bingo cards at the RSL, or in believing in stories about hairy men and ghosts? If you're reading this and you're white, you might not get it, but if you're black you will. It's a very specific kind of poor.

If you erase the part of my identity that shows where I've come from, then you erase the strength it took to overcome those obstacles. So maybe it's not necessarily that poverty is a way to determine Indigeneity, but the strength to deal with it is.

You may or may not be surprised to hear that, in an effort to overcome the specific disadvantages faced by Aboriginal and Torres Strait Islander people—shorter lives, poorer health, less participation in education and employment—the government offers special grants and programs. To access these, you need to provide what is called 'proof of Aboriginality'. There's a form you need to fill out with very particular criteria that needs to be addressed, and the form is then approved by a land council or other government authorised organisation to say, yes, this woman is in fact an Aboriginal person.

The criteria are set out on the Australian Institute of Aboriginal and Torres Strait Islander Studies website:

Indigeneity

Government agencies and community organisations usually accept three 'working criteria' as confirmation of Aboriginal or Torres Strait Islander heritage:

- being of Aboriginal or Torres Strait Islander descent
- identifying as an Aboriginal or Torres Strait Islander person
- being accepted as such by the community in which you live, or formerly lived.

All of these things must apply. The way you look or how you live are not requirements.

Government agencies, universities and schools will often supply you with their particular guidelines and ask you to complete a form or otherwise provide a letter of proof or 'Confirmation of Aboriginal and/or Torres Strait Heritage'.

So there we have it: a definition! A classification!

But it goes absolutely no way to describing what it means or feels like to be Aboriginal.

When journalist and author Ta-Nehisi Coates asked Barack Obama how he came to think of himself as black and to engage in issues affecting black people, he replied:

Well, part of my understanding of race is that it's more of a social construct than a biological reality. And in that sense, if you are perceived as African American, then you're African American . . .

I could have been an African American who worked for an international organization and was not engaged in the day-to-day struggles, politically or culturally, that the African American community faces. There are a lot of African Americans who may make those decisions, and they're still African American, but they're just living their lives in a different way.

I guess that's how you end up with a white woman like Rachel Dolezal wearing her hair in braids, emulating blackness, fighting the good fight and ending up as a chapter president of the National Association for the Advancement of Colored People. Though, by Obama's definition of blackness, it's not even based on whether you're engaged in the struggle or the fight.

There is something to be said for the shared experience of cruelty. When I see another Aboriginal person who's had any amount of success, I think, *geez, imagine what they've been through to get where they are.* Without any conscious thought, I have a bit of warmth and grace towards them in contexts where I might not for other strangers. People afford me that warmth, too. So often Aboriginal people will feel things for me even though we've never met, and I assume it's because they have a sense of what I would've had to go through to carve out the career I've had.

They know I must have experienced racism in every job I've ever had. It's truly awful, and it limits your potential in ways that are intangible and unimaginable. My heart is heavy for the people who've endured that sort of treatment after having their hopes raised with the prospect of making a meaningful contribution and making something of their lives.

I often think about the sort of racism my grandparents would have faced, and I know it's far worse than anything I've been through. That gives me strength. But we shouldn't have to plumb the depths and summon the worst-case scenarios just to endure a day at work. That is, unfortunately, what it's like for Aboriginal people.

By the way, I've been given more opportunities working at Channel 9 than I have at any other job I've been in. And I haven't had to fight as hard for those opportunities as I had to at our national broadcasters.

If we look at the number of Aboriginal and Torres Strait Islander cadets at the national broadcasters over the last couple of decades, as well as the number who are still working as journalists or in the media, we'll see that there's no problem finding talent. The problem is in retaining it. When you have to go to work every day and cop it, you start to think, *what's the point*? Only sickos like me would persevere through that. It's not for everyone, and if you've already got a lot on at home and someone comes to you with an offer where you can directly contribute to the community, it seems like most people would rather opt out.

Does it make you a bit of a sicko to be able to endure racism because you can see that there is broader benefit to it, both individually and for the community?

I remember when Stan Grant decided to bow out of hosting *Q&A* on the ABC. It felt like I'd been dealt a body blow. If this man—one of our most thoughtful, intellectual and inspiring examples—had had enough of the indignity of pandering to those hell-bent on misunderstanding us, then what chance would I stand? I felt embarrassed and exposed. Grant was willing to admit that what he had read about himself and the attacks on his family were painful enough to call time, while I was still pretending that I didn't notice I was being treated differently and that it genuinely hurt. If he was admitting that he's wounded by wilful ignorance, then I thought that surely I should be too.

I changed my mind a million times that week, constantly measuring and remeasuring the scale of my impact or the possibilities of my potential. I thought, *maybe it's not undignified to stay. There's dignity in resistance. There's dignity in the will to survive and fight against a system that isn't designed with you in*

Indigeneity

mind. Actually, it's more than that—it's designed so that we'll fail. So I decided that, while our strongest warrior has been wounded, I'll continue to fight while I can because I have to.

There was still so much work to do. Especially in a year when Australia was holding a referendum on whether to constitutionally enshrine a Voice to Parliament.

Australia is the only Commonwealth country in the world to not have a treaty or some sort of recognition of Indigenous people in its constitution. After more than a decade of consultation and deliberation, not to mention the decades of lobbying and work that went on behind the scenes to even get to that phase, the government had finally set a date for a referendum. All that stood between us and this goal was for a majority of Australians in a majority of states to vote YES. The stage was set: we were to head to a vote on 14 October 2023.

That day started the same as any other Saturday: wake up, order a coffee, light some candles and incense, and have a little stretch while waiting for my order to arrive.

As I went through my morning routine, I received a text from a friend that read:

Sending all my love to you today. You're a real professional but also very selfless to do a job like the one you've got ahead of you <3 <3

I replied:

If someone has to tell everyone NO, I'd rather it be me than anyone else

And if there's a miracle and it's YES, I want to do that too

The anticipation of hosting a big broadcast is as much work as the job itself. That's why it's good to try to stick to a routine and not get in your own head about the millions of people who'll tune in and out between the football and cricket or see clips of you on Instagram and TikTok. How Australian is that, by the way? Staging a huge, historical democratic moment in between the rugby league and Cricket World Cup.

Every time I have a big broadcast to do, I try to keep my day relatively calm. I wake up, have a coffee, do a bit of stretching and go for a big walk. Walking is the prevention and cure to every ailment in my books. It's a real luxury to be able to walk through a beautiful city with strong limbs and lungs and the ability to think clearly.

I imagine this routine is similar to what athletes do before a big game. Keep the day as normal as possible, try not to let anything unsettle you, and stay focused on what you have to do in a few hours' time.

Indigeneity

That morning, I went on my favourite walk around the Botanic Gardens and reflected on just how momentous this occasion was. This was something I'd campaigned for a decade ago. I'd made some of my best friends and biggest enemies during that time. Despite how dreary the polls were, I held out hope that Australians would gift us the miracle of reconciliation—or at least a small step towards it. I sat under a tree, looked out over Sydney Harbour, and wrote myself a note so I could remember how I felt on the day. Later on, I asked the executive producer if I could read it during the broadcast:

> Now to close out the program tonight, I have a message for our Aboriginal and Torres Strait Islander viewers. As a Gamilaroi woman, I wanted to be here tonight to deliver the results to you, regardless of the outcome. I wanted to be here to remind you all of the love we have for one another. A love that has served us for the last 60,000 years to be the longest continuing culture anywhere in the world. That does not happen by accident. This is a discussion that has at times been inspiring and at times has been ugly. We've seen the best and the worst of people during this campaign. As the sun sets on polling day, it will rise again tomorrow, and our work continues. To make sure our babies are loved, our elders are cared for and our community is strong. Yaluu and goodnight.

We put it in the rundown to read right at the end of the broadcast. At that stage, we didn't know how the night would unfold. It could take days before we found out for sure which way the country had voted. The whole week had been tumultuous; only days before we were due to cast our ballots, the situation in the Middle East began unravelling, and we were seeing pictures of people being mown down by gunfire as they ran away from a music festival in Israel and pools of blood in small villages that were dammed only by dead bodies; these scenes met with an equally grotesque display. In the face of these most extreme examples of violence and cruelty, we were asking the opposite of Australians: to show us grace and generosity so we could overcome our own violent past.

But it was too much to ask. Not even half an hour into the broadcast, the smallest state had spoken. At best, the pollsters had Tasmania as a YES, and at worst, it was on a knife edge. But as the broadcast team saw the numbers roll in on the Australian Electoral Commission website, signalling a conclusive NO from our southern cousins, we knew the referendum was going to be defeated. I sat there, my face visible to everyone who was watching on set and at home. I'm unable to disguise my inner world at the best of times, let alone when the fate of my people was hanging in the balance. I was dumbstruck, but I had a job to do. I fought back tears,

Indigeneity

compartmentalised what was happening and continued with the broadcast.

Broadcasting a live, unpredictable event is challenging at the best of times. You never really know what is going to happen, and quite often the events or outcomes you don't make plans for are the ones that end up coming to fruition. You do, however, grow increasingly skilled at pushing your feelings away so you can bring the show to the public. Most of the journalists I know could be having the worst day of their life but show up to work on air and laugh at inane jokes or do silly dances.

When there was a break, we ate pizza and listened to speeches from people like the inimitable Linda Burney, as well as checking in on all the networks covering the same event to see what they were running with. Channel 7 had a red flashing banner across the bottom of the screen that read 'NO WINS' on a loop for the rest of the night. You honestly couldn't make that up . . . NO WINS?! They might as well have had the Cash Cow dancing alongside it.

I knew what was to come would be painful, but I only felt the full weight of it when I heard Burney offer her reassurance:

And to all Aboriginal and Torres Strait Islander people—
I want to say this:

I know the last few months have been tough, but be proud of who you are.

Be proud of your identity.

Be proud of the 65,000 years of history and culture that you are a part of, and your rightful place in this country.

We will carry on, and we will move forward, and we will thrive.

This is not the end of reconciliation.

You only need to tell people to be proud when there's a reason they might not be. I sat there thinking, *would this be the beginning of a resurgence of people feeling shame about their Aboriginality?* For the last couple of decades, we'd been able to genuinely feel proud of who we are, to the point where people would claim ancestry when they didn't have it. What had we unleashed?

After the broadcast, I went home shell-shocked. More than 60 per cent of Australians had voted NO. Out of the eight states and territories, the only jurisdiction to return a YES result was the ACT.

The next day, I didn't get out of bed. I texted my boss that afternoon and asked if I could take a day off work, and he obliged. So I stayed in bed the next day too.

Indigeneity

The grief I felt was as bad as any I've ever experienced.

I was grieving not just for myself or because of the result but for the decades of expertise now slandered in the mainstream because of this toxic, doomed poll. A brilliant and resilient scholar like Marcia Langton was condemned to the side notes of this discussion and compared and contrasted with the dim wit of some others who campaigned against it.

The shift from hope to despair is a difficult one to manage. There's a shame or embarrassment to the feeling. They set us up. For a minute, we dared to dream that maybe Australians did love us. That we had moved beyond the most hostile parts of our past and into a future where we could all at least pretend that we get along. It's like Christmas at your in-laws. Maybe it's not *real* love, but it's enough to sit around a table for a few days a year and have a nice enough time.

All those blackfullas who stuck their necks out for a seat at the table were now at home licking their wounds at the indignity of it all. It hadn't been a fight; it was us asking for something from our family and being rejected. It's like when my mum would ask her siblings or parents for a loan, and they revelled in the power they had over her while she reduced herself. They wanted to know exactly how she'd spend it and exactly when she'd be able to pay it back. That kind of power dynamic is so off-kilter.

It felt like some sort of perverted experiment. Like *Squid Game*, but you're not playing only for your life—you're playing to save your descendants and honour your ancestors.

The fundamental issue was that no one who has power ever surrenders it willingly. We were asking too much of people who feel as though they have nothing to give. At the time of the referendum, cost of living was skyrocketing, inflation was high, there was nowhere to rent, and even if you were lucky enough to have saved up a house deposit for an overpriced pile, by this stage people could barely afford their repayments because of increasing interest rates. If the division started as a fissure, at some point during the campaign the scarcity mindset created a chasm between the haves and the have-nots.

I can't help but think of the quote that is sometimes attributed to Gandhi and other times to Hubert Humphrey, but it feels salient in either case: 'The true measure of any society can be found in how it treats its most vulnerable members.'

Of course, many who voted NO were led to do so because they were following advice from Indigenous people themselves. They wanted to give autonomy and control back to those whose lives would be most impacted.

I wrote about it at the time for nine.com.au:

Indigeneity

Their argument is that they don't want to be included in a document or be a part of a system that has oppressed Aboriginal people for a couple of hundred years—they ask why would this be any different and why should they put their faith in a system that has so often failed us?

They have every right to feel let down and ignored, because too often and for too long that has been the case.

I think it's fair to say that it is a complicated issue, and while there is a binary vote—Yes or No—there are more perspectives than just that.

There are some among this cohort of activists who think they know better than the people who've worked in sophisticated and delicate ways to game a system designed to see us lose. These people took up what was finite space in a debate where people had limited empathy and compassion for us, and they gave them a free pass to vote NO. It was an own goal. In the dying days of the campaign, many of them swung around to a reluctant YES, which is where those with more wisdom began. The more experienced heads had taken it all into consideration, and because of their experience and knowledge, they decided this way was the best way forward.

Many said they wanted a treaty before recognition without taking into account the impact a Voice would have had on those discussions. They also failed to comprehend that a NO vote would deliver politicians the option to be led by their electorates and abandon policies that progress Indigenous rights because there was no appetite for it among the people they serve. They now had a quantifiable reason to backtrack on hard-fought advancements, thanks in some small part to those who gave permission to other Australians to vote NO.

This cohort preaches kinship and listening to elders and ancestors, but they spoke over the top of a lot of those who have worked in these fields for decades and who know better. And it was all to make their views known and, in some cases, score clout.

It is a shame that these different opinions within the Aboriginal community were used as an excuse to further prosecute the case for the conservative NO vote. They drove home the idea that if Aboriginal people couldn't arrive at a unified position, then how was it possible for the rest of the country to do so?

By the way, I'd like to point out here that when non-Indigenous people don't agree on who to elect as Prime Minister, we don't assume that because they can't all agree, it is a sign that the government is illegitimate. Instead, we accept that there are differing perspectives and that it would be ridiculous to expect a large group of people to have homogenous views.

Indigeneity

I'm not sure it takes a sophisticated understanding of black politics and knowledge of the landscape to determine that someone with an Instagram following and a couple of years' experience traversing the complex Canberra terrain has a weaker argument or position than someone of the ilk of Marcia Langton, Jackie Huggins or Tanya Hosch. Their positions have been tested and remodelled, and while I can't say this for certain because I don't have intimate knowledge, I would assume they have compromised their positions in order to get the best possible result for Aboriginal and Torres Strait Islander people at this point in time.

However, the blame for this catastrophic result does not lie only with the population. It must be shared with those who lead them to a destination of fear instead of hope.

The most effective change happens slowly. You risk having things swing back in the opposite direction if things move too quickly. It's like a pendulum swinging: one minute you're posting a red-and-blue picture with the face of a black man as your profile picture, the word 'hope' scrawled across it, and then in the blink of an eye you see the face of a white man, also painted red and blue, wearing bullhorns on his head and storming the US Capitol building.

Recently, I've been thinking a lot about how there was that rumour about Lauryn Hill saying she only wanted to share her art with black audiences, and while she denies ever having said it and regrets that it's been perpetuated, I have had moments where I came closer to understanding that perspective and how easily one could succumb to the isolation of only communicating in spaces where you feel understood. But I couldn't do that. I want to say, 'Okay, fine, don't engage; this isn't for you,' but I can't. We don't exist in isolation. We will never live on this continent in the way we once did, where our customs and ways of knowing and being reign supreme as the dominant culture. We exist as part of a greater community.

People are scared because they don't like being on the bottom rung of the ladder. They don't want to help the people who are sitting just below them, because it might mean that they'll be the ones drawing the ire of their compatriots. They see how those on the bottom are treated, and they don't want to be in their place.

The difficult part of campaigning is being able to read the mood of the broad church and adapt in real time. To shift and manoeuvre while maintaining integrity in the messaging is incredibly difficult to do. So when the narrative shifted to the streets against the elites, it might have been more effective if the message shifted to, 'These conservatives don't have your back and they never will,' rather than 'People, be generous.' The message should have been, 'These are the same people who gave Gerry Harvey a tax break while your rent was going up and you had to stay home.'

Indigeneity

I do have to acknowledge that there are some people who just have hate in their hearts and enjoy denying justice to others. There are some people who know better and should do better, but they don't.

Some of those people might not hate you, but it's much easier for them to choose something, one thing, they don't like about you rather than try to dismantle the role they play in your oppression.

I've cried with relative strangers and heard them tell stories about how their children have taken up a place on the frontlines in the fight against racism and bigotry as the referendum drew it to the fore. So it's not just political types and the intelligentsia who bear the brunt of this result, but also children. This fight was so public and so barbaric that they now have to have retorts at the ready for their schoolyard chums. They shouldn't have been subjected to this.

Through it all, I've been waiting for a moment of levity. Waiting to exhale. It never came. Sometimes you get pulled back and, like a slingshot, somehow the momentum propels you forward. But, it seems, eventually the elastic wears out.

In the same way Stan Grant professed 'I am the old and the new', so too does the artist John Mawurndjul. In an environment where work and identity must be classified—contemporary, Australian, conceptual, Aboriginal—he defies those constraints and examines how Indigeneity straddles many genres and, in some ways, exists separately from them. He uses a traditional practice but executes parts of it in contemporary ways.

Grant's statement is a neat way to summarise being part of the oldest continuing culture in the world. As culture evolves and morphs to fit a modern context, it doesn't make the culture or our experiences any less 'authentic'. It just is what it is: an Indigenous experience, expression, identity, or whatever you want to call it.

I think a lack of understanding of how culture and identity evolve has led us to prioritise the experience of those whose past has been less influenced by colonisation, leading us down a path where we ignore the impact of our history on those who were the first affected by it. It could go some way to explaining why it was so easy for some to amplify the ideas of people like Jacinta Price and ignore others when it came to the Voice.

Years ago, my brother said something to me that has stayed with me ever since: the old people always have a plan. It reminds me of the mantra repeated in Paulo Coelho's *The Alchemist*: 'maktub', or 'it is written'. So with all the pain, the failure, the poverty and disaster, you need to make meaning out of it, surrendering to the circumstances but remembering where your values lie. You might stray from them, or disappointing things might happen, but you're on a path, and there is a plan

Indigeneity

to continue growing. For Aboriginal people, this all takes root in community and country.

Once I read something about quantum entanglement, an idea in physics that when two particles are intertwined for any period of time, they can be separated to different sides of the galaxy but will still behave and react in relation to one another. I felt as though I already knew about that concept, because that's what it means to belong to a place or a community. You're entangled forever, no matter the distance or time that passes. You're made up of the same things, and you know your impact is broader than your own experience, so you try your best to mitigate damage and chaos and promote mutual growth. Science is not necessarily the enemy of spirituality, in the same way that progress is not necessarily the enemy of tradition. They can expand and contract in a way that is mutually beneficial and so that one can feed the other.

I'm not sure I've come any closer to defining who will get what, if and when the dues are parsed out, but I know what it feels like to be in community with others. I belong to a place, and I belong to a people. Isn't that the whole point—to be a part of something greater than yourself?

Make no mistake: the result of the referendum is not just a blip on the radar in terms of the struggle for equality. It was a monumental failure and a period that I'm sure will go down in history as a time when Australia denied some of its most vulnerable an opportunity to help themselves.

I wrote a note to a dear friend when he wasn't feeling his best. I feel like we could all take something from it right now:

The world is a dark place filled with evil and horror being inflicted on those who deserve it least. Right now. Even as I type this. The reason you feel bad about that is that you're good and you know it's unfair. But just because you know about the darkness, it doesn't mean you have to live in it. The only salvation for those who know about the real evil at the core of humans is to alleviate the suffering of those around them. That's it. If you don't believe in heaven or hell and you don't think there's a higher purpose, then that is the only reason to keep on going. Because the good people have to outnumber the bad ones. If we don't, then they'll win.

So you might want to turn your back on life because you don't believe in the good in humanity, but if you go, then there'll be less of it and it'll be harder for the rest of us.

There's a quote from *Cloud Atlas* that someone told me about once. It said something like, you're nothing but a drop in the ocean, but what is the ocean but millions of drops?

And let me tell you this—we need to turn the tide so the good people stay afloat, and those who deserve to sink to the bottom.

8.

Little but Mighty

On dogs, love and loss

When you buy a pet with someone, it feels like a step towards adulthood. A milestone. It comes right after moving in together and right before getting engaged or buying a place to share. When I got my pug Reuben, I'd been begging my partner for a dog. I'd spend every spare minute trawling ads on Gumtree, and I was so desperate that I nearly got scammed a couple of times. After a few months, I found a woman breeding pugs on a farm on the outskirts of north-west Sydney. It was before we all knew about the ethics of breeding dogs.

On the day we chose Reuben, we pulled up in the driveway of this normal-looking house in the middle of nowhere we'd ever been before, keen to have a look at the litter. We were inexperienced, but the whole thing seemed gross. The dog gave birth in one of the rooms of the house, which seemed kind of unhygienic and a bit cruel. What do they do if the mother has complications during the birth or if she dies? It felt like there should have been an expert there, who could save her or the pups if something happened. The breeders seemed like they liked the pups and cared for them, but it was still very unofficial, for lack of a better word.

Despite all this, it was all very exciting. We were about to meet our new puppy for the first time. When I first picked Reuben up, he was not much bigger than my palm. When we went back a month later to get him, he still wasn't more than a handful. I cradled him in my lap the entire way home.

He was so teeny-tiny, and he'd get so tired so quickly. One minute we'd be playing in the backyard, and the next he'd be splayed out on the grass because he was so exhausted from all the effort. We outlaid so much money on the equipment you need to bring a puppy home: a new bed, toys, bowls, food. But there was nothing that could have prepared us for how much effort is involved in raising a puppy. They wake up every few hours, and you can't leave them alone for very long, if at all, in the first month or so.

We didn't know any of this. We made Reuben a home in the laundry with a comfy bed and lots of toys and thought that was enough. He came up to play during the day and in the evening, but he slept downstairs. This is one of the things I still feel guilty about. It was 15 years ago now, and I still think about how he'd howl when we put him in the little enclosure to go to bed. Honestly, I don't know how mothers of human children cope with guilt. If this is the reaction I've had to raising dogs, I cannot fathom the weight of those feelings when there's so much more at stake.

About six months later, I wanted another pug. My argument for getting the first one was that I needed a pet for company when my partner would travel to Africa and South-East Asia for weeks at a time for work. My argument for getting the second one was that the first one needed company while I was out at uni or with friends. It also made sense for each of us to have our own cuddle buddy. Sound logic, if you ask me.

Getting the second one was easier than getting the first. By then, we had a grasp on what we needed to do to keep them alive.

When we got Jimmy, Reuben wouldn't stop humping him, so we had to get him neutered, much to my ex's dismay. While he was in hospital getting the snip, they discovered that Reuben had what they called a mast cell tumour, which had to immediately be surgically removed under the supervision of an ophthalmologist. We somehow came up with the thousands of dollars required to save this little pug's life and booked him in to go under the knife the following week. I can't remember exactly how we got the money because it was so long ago, but I'm pretty sure we borrowed it from my ex's mum. By this stage, the dog travelled everywhere with us, so everyone was attached to him.

No one warns you about how devoted you'll become to these tiny creatures and how you'll coo and cry over everything they do. There are few things sweeter than observing your dog and learning about their peculiar behaviour. Like the way one of them likes to sleep in the bend of your leg behind your knee, while the other prefers to be as close as possible to your face, lying on your chest so he can nestle his tiny head under your chin. Even though you're pinned down, you don't care, because in that moment there's nowhere else you'd rather be.

Or how when you take them for a walk to the dog park, one of them prefers to patrol the perimeter and sniff the bases of trees and shrubs for evidence of other dogs in their territory, while the other will dutifully follow your every move and then, when the moment is right, run off across the park, bouncing along as if the ground is made out of that springy, spongy material they use as the base for children's playgrounds. Pure joy. You'll never spend more time at the park looking at nothing than when you have a dog.

Or what about how one of them will spend an entire morning unrelentingly trying to knock over the bin because they know exactly what's inside: scraps and snacks beyond their wildest doggy imaginations. Maybe that's where the phrase dogged determination comes from. He'd try to push it from the base, which didn't work, so he'd try another way and another way, until finally he remembered that the best way to bring down the bin and bring out the goods was to jump up to the rim and hook his paws over the top. Then both pugs were in ecstasy as they revelled in literal garbage. Empty butter containers, half a jar of nearly expired feta, leftover human dinners: all of it glorious, and all of it devoured until their little pug bellies were so round they looked as though they were with child. Two little piggy puglets, each one as guilty as the other when I walked in the door after work. I could always tell they were guilty because they wouldn't make eye contact with me. We don't speak the same language, but I knew exactly what they were saying, and they knew they were in strife. Not least from their tummies, which caused them more trouble than I ever could.

I'll remember these things about my beautiful dogs, Reuben and Jimmy, for as long as I remember anything.

I'm severely allergic to cats, so I've never really taken to them. Frankly, I've always thought people who love cats mustn't love themselves very much, because cats can be so cold and it seems like they don't really like anyone, not even their owners. They don't need you, and they seem kind of ungrateful. Dogs, on the other hand, will follow you around like a shadow and wag their little tails in appreciation of even the smallest of gestures. You just have to raise the pitch of your voice slightly and it'll send them into a frenzy. I couldn't go to the toilet without hearing a little scratch at the door—a certain pug or pugs begging to be allowed in. I guess, then, that the natural extension of thinking about cats as cold and distant is thinking that there's a co-dependent dynamic between dogs and their owners.

Did I love my dogs as much as I did because they needed me? That's an uncomfortable thought, but it might be true. For me and many other adults, having a pet will be the first time we experience unconditional and secure attachment, and it's taking place in an extremely low-risk environment, so it feels even more safe.

I'm intrigued by how the comfort and company of pets might contribute to our human interactions and relationships. You know I've mentioned that there's the stereotype about chardonnay-swilling spinsters having cats as pets, but I've never met one in real life, and all the research I've seen about older unmarried women says they're the happiest people in the world. One way to dismantle the stereotype is to just get a pug and drink pét nat.

I went looking online for some research about how pets impact us and found this on *Psychology Today*:

Eleven of the studies [out of 21] reported no differences in the loneliness of people with and without companion animals.' [Hal Herzog] goes on to write, 'The good news is that only one research team reported that pet owners were more lonely than non-pet owners.'

Regardless of the reasons people seek out companionship in animals, it seems they do have the capacity to ease the burden of loneliness and depression. This is probably due in some part to the physical reactions people have to animals: increased oxytocin and decreased cortisol. More of the love hormone and less of the stress one—the same as when you hold a baby. It rings true for me. You can't feel lonely or alone if there's a little pitter-patter of footsteps that follow you into every room. Even though sometimes pugs are so lazy that I describe them as a sack of rice with a face and tail, Reuben and Jimmy served their purpose in terms of hugs and company.

Dogs are terrific company. I'd make up songs and sing to them about the most mundane everyday tasks, like making dinner or having a bath or taking out the garbage. The most boring and onerous parts of life are filled with a tiny bit more joy, which you couldn't really express if you were on your own without feeling at least a little bit crazy. Imagine if I was at home alone singing to myself about cooking dinner or taking myself out for a nice walk. That seems ridiculous. It is ridiculous. I would never do that. But if there's a dog there to bear witness, it's completely reasonable. Lovely, even.

Dogs are also incredibly capable and intelligent animals. So what right did I have keeping them at home to make my life better, knowing full well their days were spent pining for my attention?

In 2009, the American Psychological Association wrote about research conducted by Dr Stanley Coren, a professor at the University of British Columbia who is considered the expert in dog intelligence:

> Although you wouldn't want one to balance your checkbook, dogs can count.
>
> They can also understand more than 150 words and intentionally deceive other dogs and people to get treats, according to psychologist and leading canine researcher Stanley Coren, PhD, of the University of British Columbia.
>
> Coren, author of more than a half-dozen popular books on dogs and dog behaviour, has reviewed numerous studies to conclude that dogs have the ability to solve complex

problems and are more like humans and other higher primates than previously thought.

'We all want insight into how our furry companions think, and we want to understand the silly, quirky and apparently irrational behaviours [that] Lassie or Rover demonstrate,' Coren said in an interview. 'Their stunning flashes of brilliance and creativity are reminders that they may not be Einsteins but are sure closer to humans than we thought.'

According to several behavioural measures, Coren says dogs' mental abilities are close to a human child aged 2 to 2.5 years.

I know it's not an exact science, but there's no way I'd feel comfortable with leaving a toddler at home with a babysitter without being able to explain to them that I love them and would return as soon as I could.

When my dogs were younger and they slept in the lounge room, they'd often wake up before me and my ex. They wanted food immediately, so they'd do things that they knew would get our attention and get us out of bed. They'd knock things over or scratch at the door, but these were things we could easily ignore, so eventually, after some trial and error, they discovered they could press the pager on the house phone's dock, and the only way we'd be able to stop the noise was to get up and press the button. They may not be the smartest creatures in the world, but you have to admit that was very creative and quite ingenious.

I could go on about how smart my dogs were and the silly things they did to prove that point, but I don't think I need to. We know that these are creatures with their own emotional attachments, and while I'm not sure about dog consciousness, I know they missed me when I wasn't there. Their emotional capacity was such that they could sense when we were unwell. They also had distinct personalities with their own preferences and dislikes. So why do we feel comfortable bringing these creatures into our lives when we know they'll spend a considerable amount of time alone, yearning for our company?

I thought a lot about the morality of keeping pets in the waning years of their lives when their suffering was more obvious. I can't stomach cruelty to animals, but I felt I was complicit in it by having them at all.

We'll mock people who keep leopards or tigers as pets in foreign countries but think we're above that kind of critique ourselves. I'm not making an argument for or against keeping dogs as pets, but I think it's worth considering the hypocrisy of the situation. And just so we're clear, I eat meat, use animal fats for cooking, and have a kangaroo skin draped across my lounge from an animal my brother killed himself. I'm not trying to pretend I have an unblemished record when it comes to animal welfare.

During the course of their lives, I would have spent thousands of dollars keeping my pugs healthy. I don't even want to tally the amount, because it's probably a lot.

I wrote about it for *Sunday Life*:

Sydney's eastern suburbs is the kind of place where you walk down any street and there are a lot of trees, particularly around Potts Point. They hang over the road, and only the fanciest areas have nice trees—I bet if they did a survey of the numbers of nice trees, it would directly correlate to real estate prices.

So Potts Point has a lot of trees, no children and so many dogs. The Eastern Suburbs is also the kind of place where you can get acupuncture for your dog, or have a vet prescribe it Prozac for doggy Alzheimer's. I know this because one of my dogs is on Prozac.

I'm not proud of that (well, maybe I am—I've told a lot of people and now I'm writing it here). Mostly, I think it's a bit ridiculous but I love my pug Reuben so much that I want him to feel good most of the time. And I believe he does, but yesterday he did what is known as sundowning. It's a thing: they run around a little bit confused, have enthusiastic tremors, and generally just remind you that they're close to death.

This afternoon I was walking around a suburb with nice trees and I saw a man carrying a dog in a bag with leg holes, because his dog was so old it couldn't hold itself up. It sort of looked like a hammock, but the important thing to note is the dog's legs didn't work. And all of its fur was falling out in patches as if it had mange.

Even though the owner was carrying the dog, I think the dog was also doing some heavy lifting because the man, too, looked a bit worse for wear. It was probably lifting the owner's spirits more than anything, because why else would one keep such a miserable-looking creature alive to suffer the agony and shame (apparently dogs can feel shame) of being carried in a hammock.

On this same walk I heard a child behind me ask her Mum why one of my dogs had a limp tail. It felt like a pointed personal attack. Like when a child asks an adult why they're fat or have a big nose. She shanked me right under the rib cage with her little voice.

It stung because I know the answer. He's old. Nearly too old to be walking around. Soon I'll be like that man with the dog-hammock, clinging to the last bit of warmth from the slowly dying dog like catching the last bit of sun on an autumn afternoon before the chill sets in.

Holding Reuben's tiny head between my hands as it shakes is such a heart-breaking experience. I took him to the vet to ask if we should finally pull the trigger. I burst into tears driving across the Harbour Bridge, wondering if either of my dogs were in pain and wishing there was a way they could tell me. They'd probably just ask me why they were bred with noses so squashed they can't breathe properly, or if the rumours about their brains being too big for their skulls were true.

The vet assured me they're in good health and he'd let me know when the right time was, but when I got home I found myself searching terms like 'animal consciousness', 'pugs emotional intelligence' and 'do pugs get lonely' (the last in case one dies before the other).

I've had my two pugs for more than 12 years: nearly my entire adult life. They've been there with me through a divorce, job changes, hangovers and heartbreaks. Whether or not they know it, they've been there with me through some of the worst times in my life.

I'm not weird. I don't let them sleep in my bed or kiss me on the face. But they're such interesting little creatures.

I heard a woman at the vet ask for a vegan treat for her dog and I wondered if she ever thought about what the dog wanted. Maybe it liked eating meat. Maybe it didn't want to live in her house. Maybe dogs don't even like being kept as pets. Maybe they are in constant pain. The same woman asked another in the waiting room why her dog looked so sad and she said, 'Oh, that's just his face.'

I don't know what the right answer is. What I do know is pet dogs exist to fill a void in us, but when they go they leave an even greater one, so we try to defer our grief by prolonging their lives with Prozac and acupuncture. Maybe I'll never get another dog. But then I guess I'll have to stop eating incredibly smart, incredibly delicious octopus, too.

Not long after I wrote this, Reuben died from a different disease that was completely unexpected. He was the more boisterous of the two, so it surprised me that Jimmy had outlived him. We'd started as a family of four—me, my ex, and the pugs—and now it was just the two of us.

For a while, my ex and I did what we called shared pug-stody, where we'd split the dogs' time with us equally. After a while, it became difficult to manage. People get new partners and priorities change. We'd both followed our careers overseas and interstate, so we decided they'd be better off just staying with me. I think it was maybe a bit too difficult for my ex to leave them every time he went away, so we had to draw a line in the sand.

After Reuben died, I became one of those weirdos who let the dog sleep in their bed. How could I let Jimmy be on his own? I couldn't. I also learnt that, yes, dogs do feel loneliness, and Jimmy would miss his brother just as I did. Afterwards, he'd stand in the hallway and just look crestfallen. He couldn't bear to be away from me. He'd grow depressed and didn't want to do anything or go anywhere. If there's a way to describe him as even more closely attached than a shadow, then that's where we were at. My heart was so broken for that little dog, Reuben. The little dog I carried around like a baby, letting him rest his weary little head in the crevice between my clavicle and my ear.

Not everyone understood the loss, which made grieving a bit weird. But why do people find it so hard to understand this grief? Why would they think my love for Reuben is less important than the love we have for other people? In a way, the loss was even more painful because he gave me more of what I needed than other humans and less of what I didn't.

I loved him and have cared for him and watched him grow physically and otherwise over the last thirteen years. He also loved and depended on me. Babies can't talk or interact or compel you to do things, but we love them so much. They don't make a grand contribution to society, so what are we mourning when they pass? Is it their potential? Okay, so then should we mourn more for people who had more potential than others?

None of it makes sense. What are dogs but small, furry humans that you're allowed to leave at home unsupervised?

I miss my dogs so much I would give almost anything to feel the weight and warmth of their tiny little bodies again. If you know how soft the skin and fur on a pug's ear is, then you know that pressing it between your fingertips and telling them they're such good boys, that they're angels from heaven, is one of the most precious and satisfying interactions you can have.

I had never experienced the death of something so dear before I lost my dogs. My great-grandmother had passed and that was awful, but it didn't affect the way I lived my life on a day-to-day basis like this did.

I wrote a column about it in *The Sydney Morning Herald*:

> Look, I don't want to be pessimistic or remind everyone of the seemingly never-ending dread we're surrounded by at the moment. I certainly wouldn't want to remind you of the fact that eventually everyone and everything you know and love will cease to exist—but, it will. Though, for reasons not clear to me, we feel very, very uncomfortable talking about it.

In my mind, one of the most profound utterances on the most unbearable of feelings came from the most unlikely of places: the Marvel Cinematic Universe. For those of you who think it's all superheroes and hammers, you really are missing out.

Let me explain. Wanda is a character from the franchise and there's a moment when she's sitting next to a man who would later become her husband. After she's been orphaned and loses her only sibling, he says to her, 'But what is grief if not love persevering?' No wonder she marries him.

It makes sense that grief is what love grows into when it has nowhere to go. All feelings (uncomfortable or not) mutate into uglier versions of themselves: shame into anger, fear into fight, flight, freeze or fawn. But love? The most supreme of feelings, the best thing in the world, the feeling that unites us and surely is the only point of anything, makes way for the isolating vacuum of grief.

All of us, if we're lucky, will outlive our parents. We will outlive our pets. We will change jobs, lose contact with friends and move cities—if we live our lives to the fullest. So why then don't we know how to cope when these things inevitably happen?

There's no argument here for living in a state of cat-like readiness for the next bad thing to happen, but I do think we should be better equipped to process grief ourselves and, then, to cushion the blow for those around us when they're grieving.

I didn't know about the irrationality of it. That it would take me months and months to bring myself to throw out my dead pug's harness. Even though I've moved house, and how before then it sat on the floor of my car staring me in the face every time I had to drive somewhere as a painful reminder of the love I had for the little chunk of fleshy, puggy goodness that it once held.

It's completely pointless and makes very little sense. But that is what grief is. Reluctance to make a decision that you know will probably help you. Reluctance to accept the reality of the situation: that life is happening around you and has changed in a way you didn't expect and it will never go back to how it was.

In other cultures, there are processes for mourning that help ease the burden of grieving alone. In some traditional Aboriginal ceremonies still practised around the country (in which I am by no means an expert), they paint themselves so their dead can't recognise them and can pass more peacefully into the next life. You're also no longer allowed to say their name, so they can rest more peacefully.

In eastern Australia, practices are different. Family members drive long distances from all around to hold each other in their grief. There's no formal or traditional aspect of it. I can remember, though, from a very young age the guttural sobs as loved ones were lowered into the ground. I was at a funeral recently, thinking about what purpose it served. Hundreds of family members standing there in the pouring rain and wind, listening to the wailing.

Maybe there's not much more to it than that. We're there to witness their grief and help them hold the unbearable weight of their pain. To let them allow their grief to go somewhere.

Maybe the most painful part of grief is having to hold it on your own. If love is something you do with others, maybe grief should be as well. I still have the dog harness. I just moved it from the car to a drawer upstairs.

I felt angry, and I was fighting with invisible people about how sad I was allowed to be because of my dog's death. But who is anyone to say that my grief for my dog isn't the same as the grief others have when they're mourning a loss?

Maybe the people who are critical are those who've found it easy to foster love and care and companionship in other parts of their lives, so they don't understand that this little dog has been the source of that for me for the last thirteen years. I guess it feels like what they're really judging is that I found my best friend in an animal when they've found it in humans.

All this to say, I can't stop crying about this little dog, and that makes me feel a bit embarrassed.

I've felt more guilty about my pets than nearly anything else. When I think of them, I can't think of anything else; all the blood in my body and the heat in the world flows up through my chest into my cheeks until it bursts out the top of my temples like the last embers of a sparkler. It's a relief, but it only lasts a little while—at least until the next time I think of all the times I abandoned my pets.

After Reuben died, Jimmy suffered. He seemed so much older without his brother there to keep him lively. I'm kind of embarrassed to admit it, but I spared no expense in making his life as comfortable as it could be. He had doggy physio; he went to doggy daycare; and he had as many doggy supplements and treats as he could stomach.

Reuben died in January 2022 and Jimmy lasted until October of the same year. I was completely heartbroken and depressed. Again, I cannot fathom how one would cope if they lost their baby. It must take extraordinary strength to get through the worst days of an event that painful.

After a visit to the Hunter Valley, Jimmy came home with a terrible cough, sounding a lot like an old man with bronchitis. He'd already been prescribed a ventolin puffer, which I administered using an apparatus that covered his nose and mouth, forcing him to inhale, but it was no longer working the way it used to. I took him to the vet, and they gave him some more pills. While there, I reluctantly asked, 'Do you think he's in pain? Will you tell me when it's time to let him go?'

They promised they would, but they didn't think it was time just yet. I was glad they said that even though I didn't really believe them. I'd become like the sad old man I saw at the park. Jimmy was holding me up while I was holding him up. A sad sight indeed.

By now he was feeble, and he became more so with each day that passed. In the past, after an ailment, he'd bounce back and return to a certain level of strength or health. Granted, as a 14-year-old pug, it was a low level, but there was always an uptick nonetheless.

One day, I took him to the park so we could sit in the sunshine and read magazines and sniff the shrubs (I read, and he sniffed). But this time, when I lifted him out of the car and onto the grass, he stood still. He didn't want to walk down to the best bushes. He didn't want to feel the sunshine on his fur. He didn't want to be there. I thought to myself, *the day you stop enjoying the sunshine and the best the world has to offer is the day we decide it's time to pull the plug.* I didn't do it that day—I'm not that reactive—but I did book it in for a few weeks later. More often than I'd like to admit, I thought about delaying the date further to give myself more time with him.

I sent a video of Jimmy's last stroll outside to my ex, who I've got a lovely relationship with. He replied with a message that further broke my heart:

> Omg Brooke! Thank you so much for sending this. My heart just broke! I think of Jimmy quite often and how he's doing since his buddy left him 😢. It's weird, just yesterday I was going back through photos and found one where I'm passed out on the lounge from travel and I have one pug up around my neck and the other by my side. You'd think they were the ones jet lagged! I'm feeling for you. I used to just dread the idea of these guys not being around anymore. It used to make me feel sick. I'm sorry you've been shouldering the pain of the loss. Thanks for giving them a great life and caring for them. And thanks for this pic. He's a little legend and good to see his search for the ultimate outdoor pee continues! I hope you're doing ok.

Armed with the knowledge of how difficult it was the last time I lost one of my baby pugs, I planned for Jimmy's death. I planned to get support from my friends and loved ones, and

I gave myself licence to be sad and mourn and find the time and space to get through it.

The night before, I ordered almost everything on the menu at McDonald's, and we both sat on the floor and pigged out. It's a pug's dream to eat what their parents eat, and I couldn't think of anything else he'd want for his final meal. I got him everything: a cheeseburger, fries, nuggets. And he devoured it all.

I didn't know you could get a vet to come to your house and give them the needles that put them to sleep, so I drove him to the vet and we did it there. I drove there with him on the back seat, breathing heavily and grunting the whole way. Afterwards, I drove home alone to an empty house.

There's no house emptier than one that used to be full.

Getting older and more experienced is a blessing, and not just in the hokey way women's magazines will have you believe. Every time you go through something new, you find a way through. Then the next time you go through it, it's painful and difficult, but the element of surprise is taken out of it. You know what to expect and, if you do it right the first time, you get better at soothing yourself. Actually, even if you don't do it right the first time, you'll definitely get better at it the next time you have to do it—so long as you're not a fucking idiot.

For example, when Reuben died, I felt like the whole world was caving in around me. My grief felt like gravy: thick and inescapable. I sobbed so hard I thought I was going to burst a blood vessel in my eyes. It felt like the pain was a bouncy ball coming up from my diaphragm into my throat, like rubbery heartburn that wouldn't subside. While I felt embarrassed for grieving so hard for a dog, what I learnt was that people actually have a lot of sympathy for you, and if you're in pain, most people are nice to you. I learnt that every day got a little bit easier. The gravy got thinner, until it eventually turned into water and I could function again.

So when Jimmy died, I was prepared. I knew it was a mistake to 'send it', because that would only delay and amplify my pain. I knew to have a plan to ease the discomfort in the days and weeks after. I knew that the only way to be free of the pain was to go through it. I knew that loss does change you and there's really nothing you can do about it. You can't unbake a cake. So I sobbed, I took a lot of showers, I filled up the hot water bottle and ate KFC. And I knew that it would pass.

Experience counts for something. But you only become experienced if you let the years pass without resenting them.

I guess the truth of it is that you can only really say so much about death. It seems weird or unfair that a little soul can just stop existing because the body has had enough. Surely there has to be somewhere else for it to go. But would it make it any better if it existed somewhere else? I still wouldn't have access to it.

It's true that there are no new stories, but there are new fragments to peruse if you concentrate hard enough. There are new parts of old things, new stories from other people about your deceased loved one.

Not long after I put Jimmy to sleep, I was crying—howling, actually—in the shower. It's such a depressing and embarrassing scene to recount, because it sounds so desperate and lonely, but I guess that's how it was. I sat there in the shower, tears and water streaming down my face. I couldn't comprehend that something could be there one day and not the next. How could something I'd poured so much into—love, food, affection—just cease to exist? It didn't make sense to me, and I don't know if it ever will. As I cried, I thought about how he'd normally be sitting on the bathmat, patiently waiting for me to get out so we could move to the couch for a snuggle or make some snacks in the kitchen or go for a walk and sit in the sunshine and sniff some shrubs. But he wasn't there. He would normally always be there, waiting for me. But now I was waiting for him.

Since his brother died, Jimmy had spent less of his time happy and playing and more of his time in anguish, waiting for me to get home. There was never a morning or evening where I wasn't in pain returning home, wondering whether he was still alive or if I'd walk in and find him dead. Eventually I'd find him in the bathroom, nestled in a jumper or a pair of trackies that carried my scent, waiting for me to return. Every single time it was like he thought I would never come back. I could hear him wail after I walked out the door.

I guess I just replaced his anguish and yearning with mine. Now I was the one wailing and yearning and being comforted by his lingering scent. And I still miss him so much. I often wonder if I took good enough care of him or if I could've done something to prolong his life and stave off death for another year. I wonder if it was cruel to leave him alone in the final year as much as I did. Not that I had any other option; I couldn't just be a stay-at-home dog mum, despite how much I would've loved that.

I don't know if I'll ever get another dog, not just because I'm not sure if it's ethical, but because I can't imagine another dog filling the void my pugs have left. So I don't really know what the point of looking is. I guess I'll just keep trawling the pug rescue pages on the internet and dreaming.

My dogs no longer being here was one of the main reasons I decided to go overseas. No ties, no responsibilities. No reason not to. I've got their ashes in my bedside table and have thought an embarrassing number of times about if and how I could take them with me when I go. I don't want to scatter their ashes; I want them to be with me where I'm living, because I can't bear the thought of abandoning them. I know that seems ridiculous, and it probably is, but I can't help it.

I wish I could hear the scattering sounds of their paws on the floorboards or the tiles one last time. Or the little squeak sound they'd make to squeeze out the last part of a really big yawn. I'd even settle for hearing them welp for attention one more time. If you're lucky enough to have a dog with you today, please give them a little tummy rub and a scratch behind the ears for me.

When we invite these special little animals into our lives to give and receive love, we set ourselves up for the grief I'm describing. We know their lives are shorter than ours, and so we know at some stage we'll have to say goodbye to them. It's inevitable. The alternative is that they'll say goodbye to us, and in my mind, that's a far worse situation to imagine.

In the end, I know I can't take my pugs with me. I wish I could wrap them in a blanket and take them with me wherever I go, but I know that's a really odd thing to do, so I never would. But I also can't bear to put their ashes in storage; it just seems cruel and cold. So instead, the pugs now live on a mantle at my mum's house. She wanted to put their photos next to the tiny wooden boxes, and in my mind it kind of resembled a shrine. Again, I know it sounds crazy, but I found comfort in our mutual grief and reluctance to condemn these little creatures to an eternity in a storage container.

I can't say it better myself, so I'm going to repeat the line from the MCU that I mentioned earlier: 'What is grief if not love persevering?' My capacity for love and being loved has forever changed because of my dogs, both by caring for them and by being cared for by my friends and family when they left. We think we're teaching our animals tricks, but they teach us how to sit in a park and stare at trees and the sky for absolutely no reason other than it's healthy thing to do.

So maybe that's the point of having dogs. Their lives are little but mighty. They know how to live. They make us better humans.

9.

Leaving Home

On career, chosen paths and the promise of the future

I remember my grandfather going to work in the coal mines, his shirts impeccably pressed by my nan. He'd say things about doing the best job you can, no matter what that job might be. On difficult days, I rely on those memories, as well as those of my mother taking pride in her work as a cleaner. As they toiled away in their arduous jobs, my family also supported our communities in any way they could.

I believe there is no greater purpose in life than to serve those who are less fortunate or under-represented in some way. This sort of servitude is a driving force because it gives my professional life direction and it gives me a sense of meaning. When you build out your life—your career, hobbies and friendship circles—with your values at the centre, it makes for a more fulfilling life, and it's easier to work hard because you're working towards the things you care about.

As a Gamilaroi woman, my career goals sit alongside my personal goals, which are centred around the betterment of my people. By almost any measure we sit on the bottom rung of society: high suicide rates, high rates of incarceration, disproportionate rates of child removal. A more alarming fact is that we're almost certainly more likely to experience the devastation caused by climate change than any other group of people in Australia.

To add to this misery, as it stands, the most effective mechanism for delivering policy that could offer solutions or go some way in helping to overcome some of the most concerning issues has just been defeated. The pitch was an advisory body to sit alongside Australia's parliament, which would have allowed for Indigenous leaders to have input and provide guidance on the policies that affect our people. But this idea was conclusively voted down by the Australian public in a referendum.

My goals are what initially compelled me to study journalism. Tragedy struck our family, and I grew frustrated at how the stories about Aboriginal people were rarely told by Aboriginal people. I could count on one hand the Indigenous journalists I knew, and so how could I be sure that our stories were being told with the full context and history of what had happened here and how that has contributed to the situation we're in now? I wanted to take on the challenge of contributing to that storytelling. I am proud to say that, since then, the situation has shifted substantially, and I have been a part of that shift.

If we fail to take into account the impact of successive government policies on our people over hundreds of years, then we ignore the reasons for the disadvantage we face now. And then what reasons do we have to explain the disparity in outcomes? That one race, one group of people, is better than another? I don't buy that. I can't buy that.

My cousin, Brendon Boney, is an extremely talented songwriter and musician, and one day he commented on a thread on Facebook about Sorry Day with this wonderful story, which I think about often.

> Once there were two men. One was the greatest sailor the world had ever known, the other the greatest farmer the world had ever known. Both had come from a long line before them and used not only their own skills but generations of knowledge to accumulate great wealth.
>
> One day, the sailor thought to himself, *what's better than one man's wealth? The wealth of two men!* Imagining all his dreams coming true and how amazing it would be, he sat

awake day and night, working on a plan to rob the farmer. But something else happened during those sleepless nights. Greed took over, and soon his thoughts turned to, *what's better than having the wealth of two men? Nobody else having it. Ever!* He then began working twice as hard, coming up with a plan that would not only get him the farmer's wealth but make sure the farmer never had the ability to make it back.

One night, the sailor broke into the farmer's house and stole everything. Consumed by greed, he not only stole all the farmer's wealth but also the farmer's son. Finally, before leaving him with nothing, he took out his sword and cut off the farmer's hands, leaving the sailor with the wealth of two men and the farmer with nothing and no way of ever making it back.

The sailor took the farmer's son in as his own and taught him the ways of the sailor, making sure there was as little threat from farmers as possible. He taught his sons everything he knew about sailing, and they grew up to be even greater sailors than their father. He also told his sons that if they worked hard enough like he did they could double their wealth in one night, although he left out the ghastly details.

Years later, the farmer had another son who he could not teach to farm as he'd lost the ability to pass it on. The farmer's son grew up with his father telling him, 'We were once very wealthy until an evil sailor came and took everything—even my hands to work the farm and make it all back. Now I've forgotten how to farm, so I can't even teach you.'

As the years went by, whatever the fathers had in their possession grew. The sailor's wealth of two men grew to the wealth of four, while the only thing the farmer had was pain and sorrow. Years later, the sailor and the farmer both died. The sailor passed on the wealth of four men to his sons, while the farmer passed on nothing but his stories of pain and loss.

One day, the sailor's son ran into the farmer's son. The farmer's son said, 'You're so lucky to have all of your wealth.'

The sailor's sons replied, 'Luck had nothing to do with it. Our father worked hard day and night to double his wealth. His pride is our pride.'

The farmer's son then told them the rest of the story. He told them all about the evil their father had committed to attain such wealth and to ensure all future generations of sailors would never have to rob a farmer for all their dreams to come true. He talked about how a history specifically designed to benefit future sailors was also designed to oppress future generations of the farmer's family.

Now, because of the sailor's sons' previous response, the farmer's son expected to hear, 'Wow, we are lucky. Our father's shame is our shame'.

Instead, the sailor's sons looked at the farmer's son and said, 'Well, that had nothing to do with us! We didn't do it. We're not sorry.'

This made the farmer's son feel hurt and angry. The sailors had no trouble claiming the benefits, pride and responsibility for the ancestors' successes but no such responsibility for their ancestors' atrocities.

And although technically the sailor's sons were right, they also looked like giant heartless fucking tools.

This story is such a beautiful way to describe, in simple terms, intergenerational trauma and privilege. We're so lucky to still have people with enough generosity and spirit to explain it to us.

There have been many times—too many times—where I've come to realise why there are so few Aboriginal people in my line of work. During the course of my career, my fortitude and resilience have regularly been tested. One of those occasions was when the Black Lives Matter protests were exported from the streets of the US to the shores of Australia. I played a role in explaining the Australian context to mainstream audiences who had never been confronted with these realities. I spoke about it on *Today* and wrote about it for *The Sydney Morning Herald*:

'I can't breathe . . .'

'If you can talk you can breathe.'

No, that's not the transcript of what happened to George Floyd in the United States but the last conversation David Dungay Jnr had, only a few minutes before he died with five men on top of him inside a cell in a jail in Sydney, a few days after Christmas in 2015.

He said that twelve times in the few minutes before he died.

The brouhaha that led to his death didn't kick off because he had attacked another inmate or a guard, but because Dungay was eating a biscuit and was told to stop.

So tell me again how all lives matter. Explain to me why 'come to Australia' is trending on Twitter when an Aboriginal man can die because he was eating a biscuit when he wasn't supposed to be.

When we saw that awful video of George Floyd being restrained by those officers in Minneapolis, black mothers in Australia saw the faces of their sons beneath that knee. When he cried out for his dead mother with his last breath, he may as well have been calling their names because they, too, are scared this is what will happen to their babies in Australia.

We've watched on in horror, clutching our pearls at the sight of the destruction, rioting and looting. But what do we have to lose? What hope do you have of a prosperous future when there's 20 per cent unemployment, 100,000 people around you have died from Covid-19 and police are killing your brothers and sisters for no good reason? Not that there is ever a good reason.

We've just finished celebrating Reconciliation Week here in Australia and instead of reflecting on the 20-year anniversary of seeing 250,000 people march across the Sydney Harbour Bridge in support of our enduring and impressive Indigenous history, we're seeing videos of a black kid getting slammed on the ground by a policeman in Surry Hills. We've just learnt that, surprise surprise, it was against the law for kids to be tear-gassed while they were serving time in the Don Dale Youth Detention Centre in the Northern Territory. We're seeing a 46,000-year-old sacred site knowingly destroyed by a mining company in the Pilbara.

We, on the one hand, will condemn the savagery we've seen play out in the US but sit idly by while the oldest continuing culture in the world is dismantled before our eyes.

I am all too familiar with the impact of our disproportionate representation in the justice system. So, I brought to light the circumstances surrounding the death of David Dungay Jnr while working for the national broadcaster. Breaking the story and experiencing the reaction to it wasn't the most challenging aspect—working against the tide in a majority-white newsroom was. At every juncture, the legitimacy of the story was questioned, and it was held up to a standard that seemed impossible to meet.

I am the first Aboriginal woman to hold a significant broadcasting position in commercial television. I've hosted the ARIAs (Australia's version of the Grammys), anchored referendum results, hosted the much-loved Christmas Eve carols, and been a part of Grand Final football broadcasts and fan-favourite Indigenous All Stars rugby league matches. I was the first Aboriginal person to host breakfast television when I started on *Today* and the first to cover a federal election from the campaign trail in 2013. These titles don't come without criticism from both the broader public and within our own community. There are even other broadcasters who are hellbent on trying to diminish my contributions because it impacts the way they feel about their careers. At times, this has been heartbreaking, because it's difficult to understand why people wouldn't want to celebrate the accomplishments or success of someone who wasn't really supposed to be successful.

Growing up in coal-mining country in regional Australia with my mother and my five younger brothers and sisters, the most expansive future I could dream of was securing a hairdressing apprenticeship and marrying a coalminer. In my mind, even that goal was too ambitious, because the only person I'd seen achieve that sort of stability and success was my grandfather, and I knew what he'd endured as a black man and how hard he'd worked.

Statistically speaking, I know what I have been able to achieve in my career and life thus far is nothing short of a miracle, and it is precisely for that reason that I feel compelled to help others, particularly Aboriginal people, realise their potential in whatever form that might take. I have always believed in the power of the media in helping to shape our reality and the way we see the world, but now, because of how much the world has changed in the last few years and how much I've changed, I feel like I have a contribution to make in other areas as well. I need to operate with a broader, global context in mind.

I realise that what we're experiencing in Australia is unfortunately not unique.

India is one of my favourite places in the world. The first time I travelled there I expected my bleeding heart would be completely overwhelmed by the extent of the poverty I would witness.

But what came to bear was not what I had anticipated. As I observed people busy with errands around the small townships dotted between Delhi and Agra, I saw that most people were striving for the same future. Aside from wanting a little bit more than what they have, that future consists of their children being safe, their elders being cared for, and them feeling like they're contributing to the world.

It is an obvious statement to make, but I realised there will always be people who are poorer than others and people who don't have what they deserve no matter how hard they work. In Australia, the unfair part of that situation is that so many of these people are Aboriginal, and the cause of that inequity is rooted in policy failures that are decades old. After that trip, my purpose in my career became clearer.

In the two years leading up to 2022, there was a 222 per cent increase in the number of children held in detention in the Northern Territory, the majority of whom are Aboriginal. Our life expectancy is still around eight years less than other Australians. The suicide rate for Indigenous people under the age of 44 is three times higher than the rest of the population. These statistics are daunting, but I don't think they are impossible to overcome. I have to believe there are solutions or otherwise it's too much to bear. I have to contribute to the effort to overcome them, because otherwise what is it all for? And I have to apply the same critical lens to my own work and life that I do to others. I have to share my luck with people who have had less.

Like its overseas equivalents, *Today* is the longest-running national breakfast television program, reaching 6.4 million Australians in 2023. Since I joined *Today* and the world of breakfast television—the timeslot responsible for determining the rest of the day's news, and the last bastion of untainted whiteness on broadcast television in Australia—there has been an increase in the appointment of Indigenous presenters. In fact, since then, almost every other program in the timeslot has platformed Indigenous talent.

Australia has a deeply conflicted history. It simultaneously celebrates Indigenous culture yet struggles to accept the negative impact its laws and policies have had on Indigenous communities. The senior black leadership in this country worked towards the goal of reconciliation, and a major component of that was the now-defeated referendum. I know I'm capable of playing a greater role, and I now feel compelled to do so.

When I talk about building your career outwards from your values, this is what I mean. Many people would look at my decision to leave *Today* as a shortsighted move because of how great a job it is. And it really is; I'm looked after there. But there's no point doing something just because it's easy. If you do, you won't be happy for long.

The work I've done thus far has been within organisations and institutions that hold the power to determine narratives and influence outcomes for both Indigenous and marginalised communities. This work was particularly onerous during the referendum campaign. At some point, what might have started as dog-whistling turned into pure racism. In the past, I've been brave enough to call this behaviour out or offer a counter argument, but this time I felt hamstrung by my obligations to journalistic integrity. Also, my appetite for that particular kind of confrontation and debate has waned in recent years, partly because the backlash is so intense.

I wrote a piece for nine.com.au before the campaign had even really begun, imploring the public to be educated on the issues before the campaign started and to consider the consequences:

> You should find out as much information as you can—there is a lot out there—have a look at how we've done things in the past and then decide whether you think we can do better.
>
> My fear is that nothing will change, and we'll wake up the day after and Aboriginal policy will be pulled together in the same way it always has been and will continue to be expensive and not as effective as it could be.

I supplied some stats in black and white from the government's own *Closing the Gap* reports, then continued:

It's okay if people want to vote No but I'd hope those people have a plan for what to do to improve the situation if the referendum fails and not just be content to maintain the status quo.

We also need to be realistic about how profound the impact of a No result would be on our country.

I've often reflected on how joyous it would have felt in 1967 after the successful vote for my grandparents to be able to walk down the street and know that their fellow Australians supported them by such an overwhelming majority.

If the opposite were to occur and we had to walk down the street the next day, we don't have the luxury of seeing people's thoughts, which might be 'No, but . . . I'd like to see this happen or that happen.'

What came next was beyond what I could have imagined. I'd simply asked the Australian public to approach the vote with all due civic responsibility, and what I received in response was abuse from all corners of the internet.

This kind of reaction is painful to come to terms with, but rather than be complicit or sit idly by while negative stereotypes about my people are propagated, I want to pour my energy into frontline and policy work. I hope to continue my contribution to society but just on a slightly different path.

Leaving Home

During the height of the Covid-19 pandemic, regional and remote Aboriginal communities were among the most vulnerable because of their geographical isolation and likelihood of comorbidities. However, there were no strategies in place to secure appropriate vaccines, deliver health messages to an already sceptical and hesitant population, and guarantee food security. I took it upon myself to gather with friends and offer support to local Aboriginal Medical Services to deliver culturally appropriate messaging about the vaccines. I leveraged my position on *Today*, spearheading a vaccine-uptake campaign and gaining access to decision makers, then connecting them with community leaders to ensure the food supply would continue.

It's not lost on me that finding myself in the position to do something to further the causes I care the most about is a massive privilege. It's one I intend to take full advantage of by continuing my career in advocacy and trying to move into a career that has more of a policy focus.

In the past, when I've asked myself what I can do for my country, the answer has been to build understanding between Indigenous and non-Indigenous people—to ask to be seen. But in more recent times, the answer has shifted, and now I realise that what I can offer is being part of building practical solutions to the problems we face—problems that, without intervention, we'll continue to face well into the future.

One day, we're all going to die. It is inevitable, and there's no point pretending we can evade our demise. No matter how great our contribution—unless, perhaps, we commit atrocities—we're probably not going to be remembered beyond our generation outside of our own lineages. So our responsibility is not only to ourselves but to those who come after us. We have a responsibility to be good ancestors.

People talk a lot about making their parents and grandparents proud, but what about making your children, grandchildren or nieces and nephews proud? That should be the benchmark we're striving for.

When you consider how much time we spend working to survive, it makes sense to integrate your values into your work life if you can. The average person will spend 90,000 hours working in their lifetime. A third of our lives are spent making money for ourselves and others. So what if you were able to channel your energy into a career that meant more to you and the parts of the world you care about? This isn't an argument for everyone to go out and work for a charity or move to another country to help orphans. It's a plea that I hope you hear: we only get one life, which in the scheme of things is quite short, so we should spend our precious time committed to bringing pleasure and joy to ourselves and others. If that means working in a KFC drive-through, then more power to you. I love chicken, and eating it brings me joy, so that is essential as well.

You can become injured if you work on something that sits outside of your values for too long. In fact, values mismatch is one of the leading causes of burnout. The *Harvard Business Review* lists it among autonomy and community as a contributing factor:

> If you highly value something that your company does not, your motivation to work hard and persevere can significantly drop. Ideals and motivations tend to be deeply ingrained in individuals and organizations. When you're assessing this element of burnout, you need to think carefully about how important it is to you to match your values with those of the organization.

Burnout isn't simply about being tired. It's a multifaceted issue that requires a multifaceted solution. Before you quit, really think through what exactly is contributing to your burnout and attempt to make changes. If you find that despite your best efforts, little has changed, then see if it makes sense to stay or if it's time to leave.

Putting the burden on our health and wellbeing aside for a moment, let's indulge in a little dreaming. Shouldn't we all aspire to fulfil our potential, if not for ourselves, then for those who'll inherit what we leave behind?

The easiest option isn't always the best thing for us or for the community. Sometimes we do the more difficult thing for the sake of the greater good. I've made a lot of decisions like that along the way: leaving my hometown and my family; working in industries that have traditionally not been friendly places for blackfullas, like Canberra or television.

My grandparents wouldn't have been allowed into Old Parliament House. They weren't even allowed to vote when they were eighteen. How's that for change? Two generations later and I'm travelling around with the prime minister on the campaign trail, reporting for TV news across the country.

Commercial television in Australia is a world that is dominated by a certain worldview; in fact, it helps create that worldview. When I joined Channel 9 after leaving triple j, hanging up my Birkenstocks and chucking on my high heels, I found myself in the mainstream. I was in an environment where my perspective on issues like Australia Day was completely unfamiliar to most of the audience. It was in that environment that I said I didn't want to celebrate our national day because of the unfortunate situation many Aboriginal and Torres Strait Islander people find themselves in due to the decisions that were made on that day and the days that came after. Some people loved what I said, and some people hated it, which is to be expected.

The type of leadership wasn't me saying 'screw you' to the mainstream. It was me asking, why can't the mainstream be a little more flexible? Why can't we shift and be a little bit more inclusive? It wasn't about drawing a line in the sand, and it wasn't about saying that my view trumps yours—it was simply demonstrating that we are more than one viewpoint. We are many people, with many perspectives. And we, as mainstream media, can be flexible and reflect the breadth and depth of those views.

Leadership isn't about clashing and trying to yell over the top of each other about which view is superior; it's about hearing other perspectives and adjusting your own understanding without letting it hurt your pride. This responsibility falls to us every day in the behaviour we accept and the behaviour we exhibit.

When that feels difficult, I think about the women and men who've come before us and whose lives would've been much harder than ours. Yet they still summoned the strength to push for what they thought was right. What they thought was right for us.

I've asked my grandparents about the horrible racism they endured during their lives. All their lives, they fought and they were brutalised. People would come around in the middle of the night and want to fight my grandfather because he was the only blackfulla in town. But I know they endured all of that just to make my life easier and give me a better chance.

I once asked my grandfather for advice about what to do when I found myself in situations where people treated me unkindly. He said that if someone says something racist in front of you, that's a pretty good indication they don't want to be your friend, which is their loss.

I think about all of those involved in pushing for legislative changes for Aboriginal people. They were brutalised, run out of town, and had to seek permission from the government to travel across borders. But you know what I learned from hearing their stories? And I know I've said this before, but it bears repeating: no one who has power ever surrenders it willingly. None of the gains we've made as Aboriginal people, as women, as working-class people, were ever just handed over. They were won.

If those leaders didn't push for what they believed in, we wouldn't be having this conversation here and now. That's why I believe we have a responsibility to do the same for the generations who come after us. Imagine saying to our daughters, 'we stopped pushing because we didn't think you deserved to be paid the same as your brothers'. Or to young Aboriginal children, 'sorry your employment chances aren't the same as others because we didn't adapt in the way we needed to; it just seemed a bit too difficult'. It's like saying, 'you're just not good enough'.

I'm thinking a lot about Beyoncé this morning because her new album has just been released and it's beautiful. It was born out of the rejection she felt after she performed a rendition of her song 'Daddy Issues' with The Chicks at the Country Music Association Awards. The performance was widely condemned because people weren't used to seeing women of colour being celebrated in country music.

I remember sitting in the press gallery at Parliament House one Sunday afternoon when Beyoncé's album *Lemonade* dropped. One of my best friends, who worked in a different part of Parliament House, called me, and we both expressed how overwhelmed we were feeling after listening to the album. This woman was singing about slavery and freedom and her fury at having been betrayed by the men she loved. It felt revolutionary, and in terms of her evolution as an artist, it was. *Lemonade* was a clear departure from the mainstream pop/R&B genre Beyoncé had been seemingly comfortable within for the past twenty years, and it was a full expression of the pain black women feel but is so often denied.

Not only was the album brilliant to listen to, but once I scrolled to the credits, I realised she'd collaborated with black artists from around the world, which made the project feel like it carried even more weight. Warsan Shire, a poet from the United Kingdom who was only famous in literary circles, was thrust into the limelight because of their collaboration. I bought books of her poetry because I couldn't get enough. And it turns out I wasn't the only one: sales of her work increased by 700–800 per cent because of her inclusion on the album.

Critical reviews of *Lemonade* proclaimed that it not only pushed boundaries by including multiple styles and genres in one cohesive piece of work, but that it saved the album format in an era where streaming made it easier for people to consume singles, causing artists and record companies to cater to that mode of consumption.

But pushing the boundaries of genre, style and industry didn't come without criticism. And, despite its accolades, the album still didn't win the Grammy award for album of the year.

What does it say about the limits of black women's success when even Beyoncé can't win?

This experience tells young black women that we are allowed to venture into spaces where we and our people have never been before and may not be welcome, but we shouldn't expect to win. Also, we can be the best, but don't expect the industry or mainstream audiences to acknowledge that.

My dear friend Fuzz Ali once said something that resonated deeply: 'What are young BIPOC women being told? You can shift paradigms, but don't expect to be awarded. BIPOC folks are always being told it doesn't matter. But it does. It's about narratives where we see ourselves reflected back. Those reflections tell us what's possible.'

When I think about how this applies to our own work and the environments we work within, I am frustrated and exhausted.

Race permeates every aspect of our lives. For a concept that is so ambiguous as to be almost indefinable, there sure are a lot of statistics that show if you belong to a certain group, you are less likely to succeed, and it will be harder for you if you do.

The reason I pay tribute to Beyoncé is because I am eternally inspired by her unwillingness to yield despite being denied the credit she deserves. She continues to overcome the circumstances she was born into and the challenges she faces. She stands as a beacon of what is possible in a world that wants to deny black women the opportunity to reach their full potential. Not only does she do it to succeed individually, but she also brings others with her. She stands on the shoulders of artists like Tracy Chapman and is reaching new heights, and the artists who follow in her wake will no doubt have an easier time because of the difficulties Beyoncé has faced and overcome.

It's easy to meet violence and oppression with anger and force. What's more difficult is to meet it with grace and tenderness. What these moments show me is how strong my great-grandmother was to show such sweetness when she'd only been served bitterness by the world. I think it's inspiring, and it's another reminder that after seeing so many women in my lineage be robbed of their sweetness by the cruelty of the world, I've made a promise to myself to never let that happen to me. I'll keep making that promise and I'll continue trying to keep it.

When you're designing your career or thinking about how you'd like to spend your time, it is worth thinking about whose shoulders you're standing on and who will need to stand on yours. I find comfort in taking on this responsibility. I can work harder and for longer when I know that I'm not just serving myself.

At the beginning of 2024, I knew my contract with *Today* would be ending, and as much as I love my job, I just couldn't see myself doing it for another three to five years. It's not just the early mornings, which are of course punishing; it's also the constant scrutiny and the need to be 'on' every single morning. In my opinion, it is among the most difficult broadcast jobs a journalist could do, not only because we're trying to appeal to mass audiences who have viewing habits that are only becoming more and more niche, but also because even if you're having the worst day of your life, you still have to go to work and show up like you're happy to be there. Even during the worst tragedies, the hosts of breakfast television will come to work and perform as though nothing is happening. It's a duty, and the people who work in the breakfast timeslot do it with passion and vigour. I didn't think I had that in me for the rest of my thirties.

So where to next? As I mentioned earlier, I try to build my life outwards from my values so that even when I'm feeling weak or exhausted, I'm still living a life that mostly feels worthwhile. With everything that is happening in the world, I want to be in the best possible position to be able to contribute in a way that I find meaningful.

There hasn't been a day at *Today* where I haven't felt grateful to be able to give voice to Indigenous perspectives on the platform afforded to me by the show. I felt the same way when I worked in a national broadcasting role at the ABC. But I also feel a deep sense of duty to realise my greater potential. I've reached a critical juncture in my career where my motivation has shifted away from television and towards harnessing the power that lies at the intersection of media, mass communication, and policy and agenda-setting. This is why I decided to take a year off to go study.

I don't know exactly where I'll end up after all of this. Truth be told, if I didn't have to work and I didn't feel like I had to serve the broader community, I'd probably just like to hang out at home in Muswellbrook with my mother and siblings and their beautiful children. That makes me happier than anything else. I know that seems hokey or insincere when I've written so much about travelling and celebrity and power, but I swear that it's true.

My career has given me gifts beyond my wildest imagination. But in my opinion, if you are guided by your values, then even if you're not rewarded financially, you'll still be able to do work that gives you a sense of purpose.

Sources

Chapter 1

Leigh Sales, 'Using your head to explain Taylor Swift's unparalleled success doesn't work. Her appeal comes from somewhere else', *ABC News*, 23 February 2024

Chapter 2

The Hon. Prime Minister P.J. Keating, extract from speech at the Australian Launch of the International Year for the World's Indigenous People, Redfern, 10 December 1992, p. 3

Chapter 3

Brooke Boney and Charlie Calver, 'Adam Goodes talks the Australian Dream, Raising an Indigenous child in Australia and his only regret', *GQ*, 20 August 2019

David Foster Wallace, 'Federer as religious experience', *The New York Times*, 20 August 2006

Josh Gabelich, 'Cyril Rioli: 33 reasons why we love the Hawthorn champion', *Fox Sports*, 4 July 2018

Russell Jackson, 'Former Hawks staffer Jason Burt says he "overstepped the mark" in incident with First Nations player, but has nothing to apologise for', *ABC News*, 27 May 2023

Geoff Slattery (ed.), *The Australian Game of Football: Since 1858*, Australian Football League, 2008

Chapter 4

Holly Burns, 'Yearning to be a father, but still waiting', *The New York Times*, 14 June 2023

Chapter 5

Kimberley Bond, 'Kate Winslet: "Women get more beautiful as they get older"', *Harper's Bazaar UK*, 11 September 2024

Chapter 6

Mental Health Foundation, *Body image: How we think and feel about our bodies*, report released for UK Mental Health Awareness Week 2019

World Health Organization, 'One in eight people are now living with obesity', news release, WHO, 1 March 2024

Sources

Chapter 7

Linda Burney, Minister for Indigenous Australians, press conference, extract from transcript, Parliament House, Canberra, 15 October 2023

Ta-Nehisi Coates, 'It's what we do more than what we say: Obama on race, identity, and the way forward', *The Atlantic*, 22 December 2016

Stant Grant, *Australia Day*, HarperCollins, 2021, p. 1

Chapter 8

American Psychological Association, 'Smarter than you think: Renowned canine researcher puts dogs' intelligence on par with 2-year-old-human', press release, APA, 2009

Hal Herzog, 'Can pets relieve loneliness in the age of coronavirus?', *Psychology Today*, 13 April 2020

Acknowledgements

I was so worried when I wrote this book that some of the wounds, despite being old, were still too tender to touch. I was worried that opening them up would be so painful and grotesque that it would be best if I just left them alone, but I know, and you know, that's not how wounds heal. You need to let the light in. They need to be aired out. I'm so grateful to my family for giving me the space to do that.

I was most worried about the reception from my mother. I sent her some of the book at the eleventh hour because I was so afraid of how she'd react—I remember it vividly. I sent them without warning or context in a message and waited for her response. I saw the three dots bouncing in the message bar for ages, showing that she'd finished reading and was ready to react, but the message, when it arrived, simply said 'ring me'. So I did. I thought I was about to cop a hiding for talking about things that shouldn't be talked about, about prioritising my healing over the privacy of my family. I said hello and there was silence. A long, drawn-out silence. My dear mother was crying; she said she'd felt seen and couldn't believe that I'd been able to describe how we all felt in that way. I'm grateful to her for letting me do it, for sharing it with our other family members so they could read it too before everyone else and, beyond that, for having the strength to continue to fight for herself and others. The magnitude of her strength and will to survive is something we should all aspire to.

I want to acknowledge my grandmother, her mother and my extended family. It takes a village, and despite how complicated and sometimes messy villages are, they are all a part of anything I am and ever will be.

To my little brothers and sisters—I love you more than you will ever know, and you all make me proud every single day. We have always and will always be in this together, and I am so grateful for that. I am grateful for the partners you've chosen, too; Rhian, Dazza, Sam and Joan—thanks for loving them, loving me and giving us the gift of your children. We are blessed beyond measure.

Acknowledgements

To Mark Klemens and Michelle van Raay, my agents—I would not have been able to do any of this without your support and guidance. I'm so grateful for your wit, warmth and endless patience. Whether it's live stream-of-consciousness messages during presidential debates or midnight phone calls about something work-related I am endlessly indebted to you for your experience and class. Thanks to my previous agents as well, Mark and Kristy, for their hard work and support.

To Ally Langdon and Mike Willesee for opening your home and your heart to me—I am so thankful we got put on the *Today* show desk together, Ally, because you've become more than just friends to me; over the past few years you've become family and it's been a joy to be a part of seeing yours grow too. Love you both.

To my work crew—Burlo, Karl, Sarah, Timmy and Alex. No one knows how hard you all work behind the scenes. We've been through some of the best and worst times together, and done it all with a smile on our faces. I don't know if I'll ever be lucky enough to work in an environment like that again but I'm grateful to have had it for as long as I did. The behind-the-scenes team worked even harder and created the space for us to have that fun.

To Zoya Patel, my editor, for helping me bring this together. Our incisive and lively discussions about everything from cycling to Taylor Swift and your little, tiny baby were a salve during the long periods of solitude that writing requires, and I know this book wouldn't be what it is without your guidance. Thank you.

Thanks to the publications I have published with in the past and from which I've drawn some of the material for this book—*The Sydney Morning Herald*, *Sunday Life*, *GQ* and nine.com.au.

To my friends who are a constant source of fun, inspiration and strength in equal measure—Archie, Laura, Jason, Leila, Kirstie, Fuzz, Ilai, Jinane, Sophie, Omar, Amrita, Ed, Bullant, Sarah, Al, Lorraine, Shannan, Charlee-Sue, Martha, Uma, Dyl, Roz, Bridie, Fumi, Chris and Mark.

To the dinner club—Kate, Lisa, Nicho and Toby for buoying me during rough tides.

To my friends in Europe who've given me a soft landing and been more generous with their time and space than I could've dreamed—Jen Robinson, Dave and Cort Le'aupepe, Michael Chieka, Billy, Dave and Liv, Jess Millward and the Lewises.

To the people who've supported my career and shown me that life is richer when your personal values are amplified by your professional life and who pushed me to be and do better—Tanya Hosch, Helen McCabe, Jenna Price, Adam Goodes and Michael O'Loughlin.

Acknowledgements

To my oldest friends, who've known me better than I've known myself for the better part of three decades, and who I can count on to bring light and laughter—Ashley, Kerri, Mequila, Lauren and Maddy.

To my friends in Oxford—Belen, Vaughn, Leo, Marius, Alejandro, Ana Maria, Jason, Bradley, Harrison and Hmalan. To be able to work alongside you in a year when I've had to reconcile some of the most significant changes in my life is so special, and even more special, and deeply and profoundly moving, to know how committed other people are to change and to the greater good.

To Nakkiah—I wanted to save my thanks to you for last because it didn't feel right to sandwich it between others. There are so many people who purport to be for women or mob but very few who produce work and provide fertile ground so others can experience the same growth, expression and prosperity. You are one of those people and I'm constantly in awe of your drive to make work that encapsulates our experience and also makes space for others to do the same. Your willingness to understand, truly understand and know others, is something I've rarely seen, even more so in the cases where people are busy and have to live up to certain expectations and meet needs and deadlines. It's generous, but I don't think saying just that fully captures just how difficult it must be to do and also how important it is. Thank you from the bottom of my heart for giving me the opportunity to express myself like this.

I've written this book in Sydney, London, Paris, Muswellbrook and lots of places in between. Wherever I end up, I open myself up to feeling the strength of the people who were there before me: in Muswellbrook, the Wanaruah people; in Sydney, the Gadigal people; in London, I couldn't help but think of Bennelong and his mate Yemmerrawanne, suffering and dying alone after getting on a ship travelling to the other side of the world. I stayed up the road from where they did in Mayfair and often when walking around the cobblestone streets I'd try to imagine how they felt, if they could imagine this very situation a couple of centuries later. I don't know what the answer to that is. But I acknowledge the many lands I wrote this from and the Elders who shepherded it and me to be where we are now. Always was, always will be.